The Jigsaw Journey

Allis Moss

This Book belongs to
Tim STANTON,
18, CORNWALL GDNS,
LITTLEHAMPTON, BN17 6EZ.
01903 731161

© 2014 Allis Moss
The Jigsaw Journey

ISBN 978-0-9565090-2-4

Published by MusicPrint
5 Lime Close, Chichester, West Sussex PO19 6SW

The right of Allis Moss to be identified as the author of
this work has been asserted by her in accordance with the
Copyright, Designs and Patents Act 1988.

A CIP catalogue record of this book
can be obtained from the British Library.

Book designed by Michael Walsh at
The Better Book Company • 5 Lime Close • Chichester
PO19 6SW

Printed by ImprintDigital.com
Seychelles Farm • Upton Pyne • Exeter • Devon EX5 5HY

CONTENTS

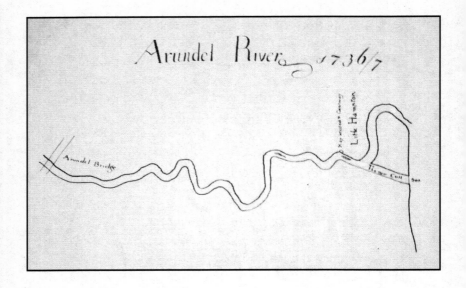

1. *Above*: Drawing of the River Arun with mouth recut

2. *Right*: Author's sketch of Littlehampton

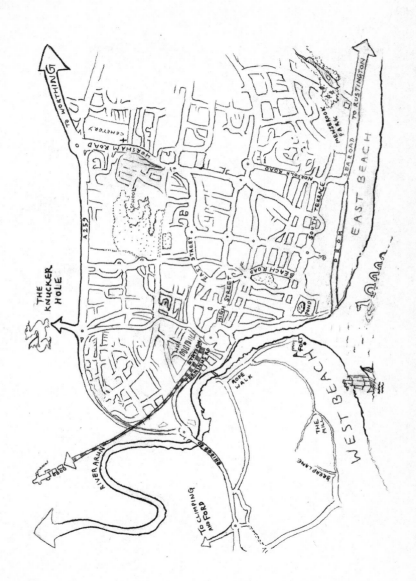

Dedicated to my late father,
Aubrey

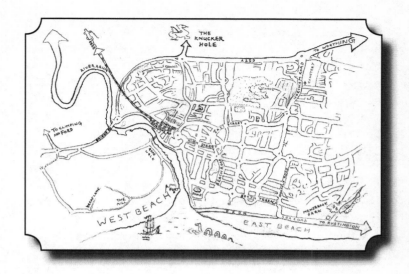

Introduction ...

Maybe you haven't heard of Littlehampton? It's a town on the mouth of the River Arun on the Sussex coast. Some who have, say it's a 'nowhereville' that might as well have dropped off the map for all its ability to lure someone not already heading there, off the trunk road, the A259. But, I found out, they are wrong.

I first arrived from the Bridge Road across the River Arun. If you turn off like I did, you have to pass the solitary gas station, with its giant gas bag inside, a pair of beautiful old pubs with their backs to the river, the optimistic Victorian railway station, dreaming quietly of its rush-hour opposite a sober stonemason's and an anonymous parade of shops. Rows of Victorian terraces, some cottages for long-gone railway workers, others with flinty exteriors, are an outpost in the town's outer layer, with the occasional cuckoo in the nest of a block of flats in the shape of a Swiss chalet. One or two of the houses have well-tended little gardens, whatever the season. There are takeaway shops, a tattoo parlour, a florist with pots of coloured heathers on seats outside, a garage offering MOTs, the ubiquitous minicab office – you know the sort of thing, you've seen it in every small town you've driven out of. The small Littlehampton United Church jockeys for position around a mini roundabout like elephants dancing on a pinhead. The roundabout acts as gatekeeper to the inner sanctum of the town, with its weekly paper, its river, its sea, boats, fun park, high street and chip shops.

Dwelling within it there are also shop-keepers, sailors, fishermen, artists, nuns, treasure-seekers and eccentrics of every stripe dwelling within it. But the teeming microcosm of Littlehampton was still in the future. How could I not think that it was in the middle of nowhere, after fate dumped me unceremoniously – in Littlehampton?

1

Sowing the seeds

"It could only happen to you," my Dad had said, and he was right. I had pulled a muscle turning the bedside lamp off in the flat in Paris that I was foolishly sub-renting from a woman who not only owed the bailiffs a lot of unpaid rent, but had longer arms.

It was a cold winter's night and I'd come home from work around 1am, dog-tired and chilled to the bone. I decided to go straight to bed instead of having a hot shower. Big mistake. My muscles were stiff and cramped from recording an obscure singer on a dodgy microphone that I'd been obliged to hold still for several hours. The bedside lamp, resting on a packing crate on the wrong side of the bed was an inch too far away. Stretching in the dark, I felt something rip in my lower back and knew I was in trouble. This was worse than having to label all my valuables to avoid their removal should the bailiffs break in while I was out.

Before that I'd been nurturing plans to cycle from France's Atlantic coast to Budapest, but instead of following international cycle Route 6 on two wheels, I was invalided out on four on Eurostar back across the Channel and eventually made it to Ford, a village just north west of Littlehampton. It had taken the ill-aimed needle of a consultant giving me an epidural to try and ease the contracted muscles in my back to turn the farce into a darker comedy. The needle hit a nerve and my leg got stuck.

So it was that one wild and windy night I arrived, not within the Danube's blue embrace, but upstream of one of England's fastest rivers, the Arun. Instead of a Parisian apartment, my new base was less a room with a view and more a room with a loo: a large, cream-painted shed, partitioned by a Chinese screen into an en-suite chemical toilet at the bottom of my mother's garden, where I now slept, since I could not climb stairs and her spare room was out of reach. But at least there were no bailiffs.

The town we now know as Littlehampton had first appeared as Hantone, meaning a water settlement, in the Domesday Book of 1086. As it grew in the 17th and 18th centuries, it acquired the prefix of Lytell – with various permutations in the spelling – to distinguish it from its big cousin, Southampton, to the west. Where cargo had originally been taken upstream to Arundel, as larger ships began unloading in Littlehampton it became the River Arun's main port. Shipbuilding and tourism took their turn in contributing, all part of the zenith of an illustrious past in what at first glance appeared to be just another smallish, faded seaside town that was busy in the summer months and in hibernation in winter.

But Littlehampton had been centre stage for major dramas. The 11th century Queen Maud, Lord Byron and perhaps the most infamous mistress to scandalise Victorian society, Kitty O'Shea, had all passed through: Maud landed at Littlehampton in a bid to win back the throne, Byron nearly drowned in one of his daring swims and Katherine O'Shea sought refuge from gossip and censure. More than 400 years earlier, one of the English Martyrs in the Catholic Church, Philip Howard, the Earl of Arundel, was caught mid-channel off Littlehampton trying to escape to France. He was dragged back to be incarcerated with his pet dog in the Tower of London before meeting with a nasty end a decade later. The man who was perhaps the most famous Spitfire pilot, Jeffrey Quill, who also flew in the Battle of Britain, was born here. Poets and princesses, mistresses and martyrs, opera singers, dairymen, peddlers from the old May fairs, smugglers, spies and bakers of pies – and, as I was to find out, dragons – have all had their business here. All of this I was to discover in the course of my higgledy-piggledy ramble about town.

Soft tissue injuries can take longer to recover than the knitting of a broken bone. It wasn't the first time my coccyx had come a cropper. From the moment I bruised it against the wooden arm of a chair on holiday in Bournemouth as a teenager, to a serious tumble from a horse years later, I had a perverse capacity to do injury to that part of my anatomy. By the time my right leg came out of its spasm, I could no longer stand on it. I was given six hydrotherapy sessions on the NHS at Bognor Memorial Hospital and also went to a hydrotherapy pool on Heene Road in Worthing, nine miles away. There, a therapist had held me and allowed me to bob in the water. The warm water cradled me, but I felt helpless. Only a few weeks ago I had been pounding effortlessly up four flights of stairs to the apartment in Paris.

As the weeks stretched into months, I slowly began to improve, progressing from walking in thick towelling socks to Crock sandals. The walking frame I had been using was consigned to the shed next to my garden room. A little gadget called a tens machine, which transmits a current through wired suckers stuck onto your skin to distract the brain and dull pain, became my most treasured possession.

I was still scared to go out alone. I doubted my ability to stay upright, so stayed near to base. I learned a routine alongside the fields of what had once been Ford Aerodrome, reciting 'lead, silver, gold' as a way to walk allowing my muscles to go heavier with each word.

My mother cajoled me into helping her to bed cuttings into a plant-holder on the outside wall of her garden. It was good to feel the compost between my fingers and to have something to focus on, but I was never going to be Littlehampton's answer to Alan Titchmarsh. To ward off boredom and frustration and a sense of being in a place out of time, I began to cast around for a new challenge.

I was still having trouble standing for long periods but had a new physiotherapist who ran a weekly 'pain' clinic. It sounded ghastly but involved massage albeit it with more needles, this time for acupuncture. My argument with the bedside lamp had now got me a needle sticking up at 90 degrees from my head.

Sue Ellen, the new physio, was a practising Bahá'í, with a penchant for both the practical and the mystical. "Don't leave the toilet lid up, else the energies of the house will vanish down it," she warned me about her guest loo in the practice, opposite Arundel Cathedral. After one of our sessions, I went for my favourite cheer-up pub-grub of fish fingers, chips and peas, then crossed the small side road into the cathedral. I love cathedrals, especially Rouen and Lincoln, for their sheer scale and the sense of serenity and industriousness.

I hobbled down the aisle to inspect the tomb of St Philip Howard. A plaque said that Philip's dog had not only been his companion in the Tower of London, but a go-between, padding along the gloomy passageways, carrying notes of hope and consolation between his master, the Earl, and other doomed inmates.

After visiting the little shop, I made my way back up the nave. On my way out, I noticed a poster, on the back of the church door. It was soliciting for walkers to join a pilgrimage in the summer along the Carmino de Santiago or St James' Way in northern Spain. I felt a spark. I'd like to do that, I thought. I'd love to do that and if I couldn't, if it was a bit too much too soon, I'd walk about in Littlehampton. The vague notion took root to walk west to east through the town, strengthening my leg as I went.

I didn't know it then, but it was to be a wayward journey in time and terrain, encountering a mixture of old-timers and newcomers, loners and eccentrics and more invalid mopeds than I had ever seen in a single town, including one with 'old bugger' on the number plate, bizarre encounters with men on stilts, on unicycles and one with a propeller stuck on his car roof such as could only really be found in a seaside town like Littlehampton. There would be a treasure hunt on the shore for shipwrecked sailors' rings, a search for comedian Ronnie Barker's seafront abode and another for Kitty O'Shea's grave, and a quest to the edge of a bottomless pool, somewhere on the town's outskirts, which legend said was haunted by a dragon that had once lived and lunched in these parts.

It didn't happen all at once. I had tried walking fast across the pebbles on the seafront not long after my arrival, but it was too much, too soon. A pain erupted like a 'crown of fire' on my right knee and the next day I could barely walk. You need to learn more patience, I was told. I had already tried potting plants. Now I bought a block of Das modelling clay in its silver foil, but didn't open it. I was keenly aware that one minute I had been living in a chic flat in Neuilly-Sur-Seine working a Metro ride away in a Paris newsroom, the next, bedded down in my mother's garden. I followed the oval perimeter of her flowerbeds, as spring blossomed with early roses, camellias, clematis and mimosa, walking with a pile of books balanced on my head as Sue-Ellen had instructed, as if I were a debutante at a Lucy Clayton finishing school, one of my mother's dogs, a corgi-cross called Bertram, accompanying me at a playful gambol on his stout little legs.

Bertram was a Dr Jekyll-and-Mr Hyde corgi-cross unfit for a queen, alternately regarding me as if butter wouldn't melt in his mouth, then metamorphosing into a control freak. He was nothing if not entertaining. We formed a close bond in those months, where he was the companion to my recovery more than any human. I eventually graduated from circuits with Bertram in the garden to a bracing stagger along Littlehampton promenade, deposited by friends' cars at a public bench on Sea Road opposite the Victorian-towered and cupola-topped convalescent home. The bench was my launch pad to my ultimate goal of a plaque recording the air speed records set here. I walked up and down the prom, with more strength and confidence and going further as the days passed. I kept a weather eye on other individuals plainly recovering from hip operations and the like, emerging on their new crutches, on the other side of the road. It gave me a ludicrous sense of satisfaction if I outpaced one of them. Sometimes I made it as far as a little brown hut, and soon I reached the stone marker to the world air speed records in the parish of Rustington. On September 1946, Teddy Donaldson became the first person to break the 1000km an hour barrier in a Gloster Meteor Star plane. Six years later, another airman Neville Duke, set a new record in a Hawker Hunter WB188. Duke himself unveiled the little stone plaque on the anniversary of the first record when both aircraft flew over the spot again.

To me, it seemed a rather unlikely place for world records. There was a shelter to sit under at the top of the beach that was popular with ravens, a number of the glossy-winged birds always pecking among the pebbles.

Finally one afternoon, I caught a number 700 bus into Littlehampton's Anchor Springs where the town's old brewery ued to be and headed for the public library in Fitzalan Road, where the quietly-purposeful air wrapped itself around me. 'Free Library' declared the stone plaque, with its ship, pier and lighthouse, over the doorway. The spirit of the Victorian age enshrined in the town's motto had become my own: 'Progress.'

2

Wild West Beach

It was many months later on a Sunday in January, as the rain battered the roof of the garden room, that I started to map out my jigsaw journey route to take in the river, seafront and town. I had already decided I would walk each leg like the piece of a puzzle. It couldn't be linear, of course, as the area needing to be covered was too small, even for someone recovering from an injury. I would work my way from west to east along the seafront, doubling back into the town with the proviso that rules are, of course, made to be broken.

When I set out to walk my first piece in the jigsaw, it was a freezing afternoon in early February. My destination was West Beach. The first piece of the puzzle was an ambitious loop along the sand dunes to a stone tablet that officially demarcates the town boundary at Climping Gap. As some six months had passed and I was now able to drive short journeys, I parked in the West Beach car park where the café was shuttered for the winter, apart from weekends. Offers of hot food on a menu board made my mouth water.

Cocooned in a pair of bright-orange earmuffs, I set off, feeling I should perhaps have some Kendal mint cake with me instead of the notebook, pen and map stuffed in my coat pocket.

I hadn't taken more than a few steps when I realised I wasn't alone. Despite the lack of refreshment from the shut-up cafe, a few other souls had been drawn, like me, to West Beach and one of them was at least ten foot tall!

"What on earth are they?" I shouted up, too agog to care that I was interrupting the thing's mobile phone call. This half-man, half-robot towering above me was a local gent on high-tech stilts. Moments later he introduced himself as Gary from Wick. Gary, who was to be one of a trio of Garys I was to meet on the jigsaw journey, ended the call.

"They're pro-jumps," said Gary from Wick, indicating his stilts. "If you run in them you can do 25 miles an hour – as fast as a car. But I've only just started, so I'm sticking to walking." And off he tottered, walking but not running, in a vision as surreal as it was unexpected.

"Did you see that guy on those incredible stilts?" I asked a twitcher who'd appeared out of the gloaming in a deerstalker with a pair of binoculars round his neck.

"I thought he had a disability," he replied. I hoped he would have better luck identifying the birds.

Just ahead, a woman with two dogs and a puppy in tow

was collecting driftwood for firewood, or so I thought. But Donna was a sculptor of sea-art and was searching out logs that had been "blessed by the sea", gnarled and beautiful chunks of wood that had already been carved and patterned by the waves.

"I use pegs to make wood sculptures, then paint them," she told me.

I waved goodbye and began tramping over the shingle at the highest point alongside the dunes. I was heading for the point below where Mill Lane meets Bread Lane, from the days when the mill produced the local flour for baking the loaves on which Littlehampton marched. The dunes stretch for miles, built up over time by the long-shore west to east drift. As I was high up, the sea was sometimes blotted out so it seemed the peaks of the dunes met only cloud.

I reached the stone tablet at Climping Gap, raised on a dais like Aslan's stone table in Narnia. A pockmarked sign in need of a lick of paint with half the words missing, and another with faded lettering, proclaimed West Beach as an 'Area of Special Scientific Interest' with triple status. Ringed and grey plovers and birds of prey such as kestrels and oystercatchers haunt these beaches. While below, in the teeth of wind and tide, life flourishes in the dunes from sea bindweed and periwinkles to hare's tail grass and tamarisk, from the lugworm to the yellow-horned poppy.

With the tide out, I decided to walk back to the car along the exposed wet sand of the beach. The Environment Agency had removed a load of shingle from the beach, so it shelved dramatically and the high water mark came right up to the top of that shelf. Go back even further, to around 80 years ago, and there was no shingle at all. It was brought here to shore up the beach defences.

Years before, I had gone to the beach below the cliffs at Saltdean, some 40 miles east of Littlehampton, to record my first ever radio feature on a search for fossils. An experienced geologist had accompanied me, armed with a hammer, to crack open pebbles to look for the fossils within.

"Pebbly beaches can be so much more interesting than lovely soft sand," he had said. We had become engrossed in the task and the interview had come to an abrupt end with us both having to climb over a concrete groyne to escape the incoming tide.

Mindful of the high-water mark here, I quickened my pace. The huge bleak winter sky sank through lavender to a chill grey. The dunes and sky felt immense and on the edge of this island. Night hovered. I bent down and selected a smooth chunk of wood with delicate criss-cross tracery on it to take home. There was just enough daylight to return to the car park. From there, the beacon of the odd-shaped lighthouse tower juxtaposed next to the pointed turrets of Harbour Fun Park's fairy tale castle, on the other side of the river, was like the edifice of some strange Star Wars planet. The out-of-season illuminations of Littlehampton's promenade lighting up the other side were swinging forlornly in the wind. I was looking forward to a cup of coffee and a hot bath before doing any more pieces of my jigsaw journey.

*

I returned early one bright wintry morning to find out more about the flora and fauna on West Beach. Daphne and her team of volunteers had just finished litter-picking on the beach. A former ranger and parks officer, she was a mine of wondrous information. She knew that the grass on the boardwalk by the car park grew lush and vigorous from a potent manure of dog poo and ice cream. She could tell the difference between a dogfish and a ray egg case. She knew that the caterpillars kept the ragwort down. That the feisty little plant with honey-scented leaves growing valiantly on the upper part of the beach was sea kale, with roots that burrow down like Marram grass many feet deep into the shingle. Sea kale is an ancestor of the cabbage and in Littlehampton Museum there is a recipe from 1790 about how to cook it. It was hugely popular in the eighteenth century and, having been depleted as a free snack in the past, is much rarer now. Then there are the oysters from Chichester Harbour. Daphne explained that where you find prey, you always find predators. Living close by the oysters were the oyster drills. They are both molluscs, but the drill feeds on its food by injecting it with a bit of its shell then digesting it. Millions of pink slipper limpet shells on the beach are an invasive species that came over from Canada in the 1890s and have an interesting sexual habit. They form chains on the seabed of alternating female and male shells. When one dies, the next one undergoes gender reassignment and obligingly changes sex.

Daphne showed me how to identify the ray's egg cases that we call mermaid's purses and told me the things I'd thought were sponges were actually whelk egg cases. There are genuine sponges down on the beach, too, that come from Bognor Reef, where on summer days Daphne said you can get great snorkelling at low tide.

For Daphne, the best sight in Littlehampton is the cormorants. "You can see them diving into the sea for fish and sitting on the pier drying their wings afterwards." She pointed at one that seemed to be doing just that. "They're just like little dragons, stretching out their wings, basking in the sunshine. You can sometimes see a whole row of them."

But we saw only the lone cormorant that morning. I was disappointed not to catch sight of the sand lizards introduced to West Beach a few years ago. They go bright green in the breeding season, while in spring the dunes turn into a haze of blue, carpeted by forget-me-nots.

3

Fort for the day

A few days later, I eyed up the target in my next mission, or, at least, what I could see of it: the Napoleonic fort on the mouth of the River Arun, its fate intimately entwined with the dunes. But first I had to get in – and on it; a man called Gary Baines was going to help me. I had a rendezvous with him on this side of the barbed wire. Gary was definitely a popular name in these parts. First there had been Gary from Wick on his high tech stilts. Now there was Gary Baines, who was almost as tall without any stilts. And there was more to follow.

At 6ft 5ins tall, Gary Baines was the manager of an amusement arcade. As soon as I clapped eyes on him, I knew no one would ever try leaning their weight against a one-armed bandit to get a row of lemons while he was around.

But Gary is a gentle giant who sees all of life in the arcade, winners and losers and every shade in between, including a man who lost everything and had to move from his five-bedroom house into one room. Inside this microcosm of humanity, Gary would take a book on his favourite subject of coastal forts to read whenever the arcade was quiet. He has become the guardian of various forts along the Sussex coast. He likes them because the last place he went with his beloved granddad was a fort and Gary had fought hard to gain recognition for the one on Littlehampton's West Beach.

It is one of the town's best kept secrets, since it is shrouded in foliage and mystery and half-buried in sand – after being blown up to boot. Built by Littlehampton men under the direction of Captain Fenwick of the Royal Engineers its role had been to replace the old gun battery on the east bank and it had never been defeated by the enemy. What was left of the old fort has only ever been conquered by nature. It had gone down in a barrage of ivy and was now captive in a forest of creepers, like something in the pages of an illustrated bumper book of Grimm's Fairy Tales an aunt had given me as a schoolgirl.

"No one would even know the West Beach fort is there," Gary told me. "It's hidden not only by the masses of ivy, but by the banks of sand dunes that have built up over the years."

The fort originally commanded panoramic views of the sea but the marshy land behind it has since been transformed into a links golf course. It is now below the level of the same sand dunes that host the sea kale, lizards, yellow-horned poppies and forget-me-knots further along the beach. The prevailing Westerlies, blowing west to east, have driven sand across the interior of the open ruin and up against its easterly wall over the years, so that more than a dozen feet of sand have accumulated with vegetation growing its roots down into it. In the past, Gary has worked with a ranger to trim the ivy back to expose the gun emplacements in the walls so that the foliage resembles an eccentric thatch.

I watched Gary crawl under barbed wire onto the links golf course. There was 15ins more of Gary than me, but he managed the challenge easily and had obviously wriggled this way before. Nor were we trespassing, as Gary had the permission of the golf course to monitor the site. I was not exactly that good on my feet at the moment, but I was okay on my belly. I followed suit.

Gingerly, I stood up again and brushed myself down. A 15ft ditch that used to protect the fort's outer wall was now filled with wind-blown sand, so we'd emerged from under the barbed wire almost level with the top of the outer wall. In front and above us were the surviving ramparts – all the French would have seen had they ever attacked Littlehampton from the sea.

The fort and gun battery built some 90 years earlier on the other side of the river owed their existence to an ever-present threat from the country I had so ignominiously retreated from the year before. That threat had continued under Napoleon III, the original Bonaparte's nephew. Napoleon junior reinvented himself as Emperor of France and sent secret agents to spy out the lie of the land across the Channel. In 1854, two years after the new Boney was crowned in Paris, Littlehampton built the replacement fort.

The French spies reported back that neighbouring

Portsmouth's seaward defences were impregnable, but the port was vulnerable to attack from the rear. If they could sail up the Arun and land at Arundel to take the great naval port from behind, the French army would march on London. But in the end, Napoleon chickened out of using Littlehampton harbour to mount an attack on Portsmouth. In any event, the attack never came and the south coast forts, of which Littlehampton's was the first, acquired the nickname of Palmerston's Follies after the prime minister had so 'foolishly' ordered their construction.

Now Gary and I stood between the ramparts and the 'Carnot' wall, perforated with loopholes that you can still see, to fire musket balls at the French. The open-walled design had been the fort's Achilles' heel as an attacking army could have peppered the sentries with grapeshot – the metal slugs packed in canvas bags fired from cannons at the time. Later forts had closed-top 'caponiers' to protect the men guarding the ramparts.

We inspected the slits for the rifles, then it was time to negotiate the ramparts trampling over three or four feet of ivy and brambles. The brambles were much deeper where the gun emplacements and cannon had once stood. Some of the ivy tendrils were like lassos, and I had an image of being torn to shreds as I plummeted down where the ivy had gone rotten into its dank heart. But nothing more dramatic happened than being scratched by thorns.

Although ammunition was never used at the fort in anger, one soldier died there in the 1860s or early 70s when a man was accidentally shot with a rifle while training. He survived – but the one who shot him died of shock. The event is chronicled in West Sussex Records Office in Chichester. Another legend surrounding the fort tells the story of a soldier returning from the Boer War who was too traumatised to live in normal society, so made his home with the garrison.

"And is yet to leave," Gary said darkly, referring to tales of the fort's ghost.

There were no soldier ghosts that day. The sun was high in the sky and shining full in our faces. Thanks to Gary's efforts, English Heritage has declared the fort 'an ancient monument'. Local policeman Andy Orpin has since taken over where Gary left off. It is now illegal to build on the fort, dismantle it or cause wilful damage. I hoped that one day it would be visible and accessible.

On the golf course, one or two chaps were teeing off. In aerial photographs you can see the layout of the fort including the soldiers' quarters, cookhouse and privies. But only the outer defences remain. The barrack block that once housed the soldiers is long gone. In its place, I saw a parched patch of grass where the doors had once been. What happened to the barracks is a mystery. Gary Baines will tell you how a hundred years after it was built, the Christmas Eve edition of the *Littlehampton Gazette* carried a story that the fort was going to be demolished. The job was apparently to be done by a company called Pages Demolition. But when Gary tracked down Pages' elderly boss many years later, the man insisted his firm hadn't done the job. Someone blew up the barracks in a controlled explosion. Whodunnit? The question is still unanswered.

4

Walking the Rope

I was hunkered down in a corner of the long road of Rope Walk's only café, having taken refuge from a sudden squally hail storm. There was a large helping of scrambled eggs in front of me and 'golden oldies' on the radio as hailstones tattooed their own drumbeat on the shop sign outside.

Rope Walk is at the end of Ferry Road, curving off the main coast road of the A259 after it crosses the Arun near Tesco's and sweeps past fields to rejoin the river. People say the name Rope Walk comes from 'walking the rope' or teasing out the rope as you're making it. It's a long rope to tease out, hugging the river all the way down to Gary's fort. Wharf Road and the main part of town are on the other side of the river reached by a footbridge. Here on the Rope End of the bridge there were twin stumps of green lamp-posts from an older bridge. Like the stone dais on West Beach, there was a whiff again of Narnia and the lamp-post marking its outer boundary among the fir trees. I was finding Littlehampton's otherworldliness strong here in Rope Walk with its single 'bed and breakfast' sign and general air of abandonment.

The café had its regular busy times with workers from the offices and the boat repairers from just down the road who always came in for breakfast. Just then it was gone three in the afternoon and I'd missed 'last orders', but Jan had kindly scrambled four eggs-on-toast after hearing I'd had no lunch or breakfast worth mentioning. The café, then called Ma's Kitchen but about to change, had recently been taken over as Ma had gone south to France, said Tina, the waitress, who had herself moved south, but in her case from Crawley to Littlehampton.

"Best move I ever made, with the river and beach, and everyone here so friendly," she confided.

Jan wiped her hands and came over from the kitchen to join us for a gossip. "I lived in Worthing for eight years without ever once exchanging a word with any of my neighbours," she said. I learned that where the old boatyards used to be in River Road, a smart new restaurant, part of a residential block, had opened and Jan's fella worked in the kitchen.

Next door was Davis's Chandlery, written with a small second 's' on the outside window of the diminutive corner shop. Inside it was a tiny curiosity shop, an Aladdin's cave filled with tins of paint and varnish remover, bottles of turpentine and linseed oil and jerry cans with balls of twine and wire wool and tackle for treasure. Shelves were lined with cans of silicone lubricant and yacht primer and boxes of screws in every conceivable space.

"My nickname's 'the Old Bastard'," chortled Peter by way of introduction after I went in to explore. His face took on a doubtful expression. "Perhaps you'd better play safe and just put the 'Old Bugger' if you write it down," he added as an afterthought, laying aside the copy of the *Sun* he'd been thumbing through, declaring, "ten or 15 years ago, business was booming and I wouldn't be sitting here talking to you." Peter was sunbathing in a wooden chair in the now sunny shop window. "Now you could sit in the middle of the road and not get knocked over. It got worse after they knocked the old bridge down. After that, as the generations changed, people don't know we're here, in Rope Walk."

"What was it like when you first came to Rope Walk?" I asked the Old Bugger.

"It was a gravel road with potholes large enough to bury half a car in and no street lights. The main sewers had only just been put in. This place was on a cesspit at the back. There were always mobile homes. Half-a-dozen people were living in old converted buses here." Peter paused and laughed at the memory. "My governor said, 'There's a lady over the top north side with a converted single-decker who wants some bunk beds put in – I'd like you to go and measure it and do the job for her'." Peter made a face. "She had goats and the place stank like hell – it was the fastest job I ever did."

Another feature of Rope Walk was its wooden chalets. One Peter knew of was built up over the entire chassis of a British ex-army First World War lorry, complete with steering wheel, engine and solid tyres. The lorry was still there. The chalet had simply been built on top of it.

Such delicious eccentricities would no doubt be swept away if hundreds of new homes were built here, something that was down as a possibility in the Town Plan. However, without flood defences, prohibitive costs would mean it was unlikely to happen any time soon.

Peter had other yarns for me from his Littlehampton past in the shop that afternoon. He told me about the Little Red Bus of his childhood that had served the town along with the village of Burpham and Arundel when he'd been a schoolboy at Groombridge House in Norfolk Road. The bus had been driven by an enterprising gentleman with sharp business tactics.

"He'd wait in Arundel square," Peter grinned remembering it, "then pull out in front of the rival Southdown bus and steal a march on it and all its passengers!"

Peter's schooldays had ended when he was 13 at the end of the long summer holidays when his mother, a teacher, had told him to get ready for the new school term.

"I told her I wasn't going back. I'd seen a sign saying 'boy wanted' on a launch. I went in and got the job." Peter made tea for the men and helped out generally in the yard. During the Second World War, he was still there, when the yards had to stop making the yachts they'd been famous for in the 1930s and turn, instead, to producing lifeboats and boom boats for the Admiralty, gunboats and motor launches for the Royal Navy and oars by the truckload for the merchant seamen.

In the shop, we traded war stories. Mine was my Grandpa Joe, who had first shown me as a child how voices from faraway could come out of a box in an old wireless. Grandpa Joe was a fireman during the London Blitz and had fallen out of an upstairs window in the act of rescuing a woman from a burning building. Peter remembered a plane flying low over Littlehampton seashore. "I only realised he was a bomber when he released his payload onto the golf course."

"Did he get a hole in one?" I asked and Peter was good humoured enough to laugh. He'd been an 'essential worker' with a team of women all toiling for the war effort making light, reinforced ladders for the Fire Brigade, including possibly the very one Grandpa Joe had missed his footing on. Drafted into the Home Guard, Peter had been allocated a billet in the Arun View pub and ordered to guard the iron bridge across the river in case the enemy tried landing under cover of darkness.

"The most frightening thing was the cows rattling their chains in the cow shed opposite the cemetery on the Horsham Road. It was very loud that night," Peter confided. Later the Navy had allowed him to enlist as a shipwright.

He told me how, ashore one evening, he had just finished eating supper with the other sailors in a dining room above a shop.

"When I left it was pouring with rain. I dashed into a Burton's menswear store, knocking into these two girls." To make amends, he took them both out for supper. He later married one of them, an American. "I was a GI bridegroom," he chuckled. A day after the wedding, the newlyweds came to live in Littlehampton's Clun Road. Peter eventually returned to the yards working as a chargehand and foreman, then designing and building small motor cruisers for William Osborne's.

"A boat came off the production line every two weeks," he said wistfully. "We all had our specialities. Osborne's was known for a fine finish, Hillyard next door for their famous wooden yachts, good, strong, tough sailing boats. Osborne's made the prototype for every lifeboat. But the end came when the lifeboats dried up," he said with a note of finality.

*

I set off, heading as Peter had directed, for the upper or lower road to the beach. I passed a sign offering free winter storage, while another on the gates proclaimed itself as 'The Shipyard': Moorings – storage – slipway – scrubbing. Out of season, the B & B had no vacancies. I passed Wym Engineering, Osborne of Arun and Littlehampton Yacht Club, all housed in Rope House, then Dutton Amphijeeps, one of the small white jeeps with its boat-shaped bonnet, was parked out in front. I felt I could have been anywhere remote from Newfoundland to John O'Groats. Anywhere that had that solitary air and a feeling of being on the edge, an in-between and peripheral place.

I took the Upper Road with a view of the bank and the mud with the odd tyre poking up and the skeleton of a hull looking like a miniature Sutton Hoo, the Saxon grave ship. It was easy to see this had once all been marsh, before the course of the river was altered. Aware of the little suckers of the tens machine buzzing on my back, I passed the Wendy Ann 2, Arun and Littlehampton's yacht club houses, a lovely lone house then a small metal bridge.

The bridge led to Teddy Butler's Island. Peter had told me about Teddy Butler. When Peter was a lad before the War, he – like everyone – knew Teddy. A short and slightly tubby man, Teddy was famous for always wearing his dark, peak cap. He had a little workshop on the island, where he kept piles used for working in the harbour on boats to be inspected in the mud docks. The girders for the bridge, Peter had told me, had come from the old market in the town, promising to put me in touch with Dean 'Deano' Kelly who had once run it.

Two anglers were engrossed in setting up their rods at the top of the beach. I asked what they were hoping to catch.

"Sea bass," came the reply from one, followed by the pessimistic postscript: "but I've never been lucky."

"You will!" I laughed in reply.

You don't realise how lovely Littlehampton can be until you come to Rope Walk, and go down Ferry Road and the upper road to the boardwalk. You take in the sweep of the beach in all its gilded majesty. You begin to see that Littlehampton has rare gems, not strung out artificially on a necklace, but occurring naturally, studded here and there, precious seams and pockets running through between sea, river and town.

A cloud like a slab of concrete hung in the sky, backlit. Dogs raced on the sand, one of the hounds, newly unleashed, chasing seagulls in ecstatic delirium. A family of three stood at the water's edge, the toddler a defiant silhouette erect as a miniature Canute watching the sea roll and toss itself against the wooden structure of the West Works. A lone bird ran along the lower level of the Works, pecking like a cartoon woodpecker. At the end of the upper level beam, several cormorants were huddling like a group of shy pensioners at a tea dance. Sand grains blew in the breeze like fairy dust. It was suddenly impossible not to feel happy.

*

On the way back, I spied the fort, covered by its green fuzz of ivy, only glimpses of its Carnot wall visible. The lovely house had a beautiful pair of gates, fashioned out of wrought iron and dried reeds. Golfers were out on the sunlit greens. The club house weather vane, in the shape of a golfer, creaked in the breeze. Voyeuristically, I watched a golfer miss a short putt. A solitary cyclist passed me. Rejoining the upper road, I could see the orange lifeboat launch with three men aboard setting out on a call somewhere. The launch stopped en route to inspect a mooring then sped out towards the harbour mouth and out of sight.

5

The not-so-nutty professor

After a short lull in my walking I picked up my route a few days later at the footbridge. Long ago, before there was any ferry and when the only bridge was higher up the river at Arundel, passengers were rowed across. If you had a horse, it had to swim tethered to the stern of the boat.

I had paused on the Rope Walk side of the new footbridge to read about the Lapstone, also known to locals as Noah's Ark, a nineteenth century smugglers' dwelling berthed permanently on the river in front of the Arun View public house until the building of the Swing Bridge at a cost of £13,000 in 1905 moved it on. That bridge was in its turn replaced by a modern road bridge and now there's only the footbridge, which is retractable so commercial shipping or vessels with tall masts can sail through.

I walked across the footbridge, stopping midway to look at the uninterrupted views up and down stream. A woman pushing a buggy, with two toddlers in tow, passed me going in the opposite direction. At the Wharf Road end of the bridge, there was the sharp tang of Arun mud exposed by the tide to the hard winter sun. At this end there was another mottled plaque. I saw it paid homage to a long-ago drama from the days when a chain ferry plied the Arun. During one crossing, the chain had snapped with a parson from Ford aboard, the ferry swinging out dangerously on the open river. I knew there was a brand new ferry now but it was winter, so in dry dock, as it operated only in the summer months.

I stood, hesitating outside the two splendid-looking pubs which were riverside neighbours. Although just a short distance apart, the Steam Packet was on River Road and the Arun View on Wharf Road where the 'Old Bugger' had once been billeted. The Steam Packet, where railway workers used to escape for a swift pint, was newly painted a fresh duck-egg blue and would soon be open for business again, offering real ale and accommodation. I made up my mind to try both pubs, starting then and there with the Arun View, promising myself I would return to try the Steam Packet another time.

"Chips or potatoes?" enquired the friendly waitress after I'd settled in a window seat overlooking the barnacle-covered fendering of the bridge, around which swirled the Arun's waters, a deep, inscrutable green.

"I'll be good," I replied with a hang-dog expression, then asked to borrow her pen to write up my notes as mine had run out. In no time at all, a delicious piece of plaice, filleted and grilled, with the carbohydrates boiled beside it, was placed in front of me. A succession of waitresses appeared to ask if I wanted tartar or tomato sauce. Perhaps they thought I was a restaurant critic, or worse, a health and safety inspector. After wolfing down the main course, I decided I might as well be hanged for a sheep as a lamb and followed it with homemade plum and apple crumble for pudding. It was fully dark when I stepped out of the pub and a train was just pulling out of the station. A young man with a mop of curly dark hair strode past carrying a backpack and a guitar passing the Steam Packet, reminding me of my younger self. It wasn't only the town that had layers of former days. I watched his retreating back, wondering what dreams he had ahead of him and which would come true. I knew well that we have several lives within the one we know of. I shook myself. I had an appointment with a professor.

*

In Roman times, Arun's name in the Celtic tongue was Trisantona, meaning Great Wanderer, which was later corrupted to the 'Tarrant'. It seemed to have lost its two 't's since then. Several attempts had been made to pinpoint where the River Arun had run before it was effectively made a canal in the 1730s. It seemed the Arun had shifted its course more than once, as it silted up, finding its way to the sea.

The oldest surviving map of the river was a copy of an earlier one drawn up in the 1600s. In the Middle Ages, the village of Atherington, still marked on my AA map, existed to the south of Climping. The old Arun must have run east of the now lost village in medieval times. I was told by some who knew it well that you could still see the lines of the old dried-up channels on the western side of the river. The district council's coastal engineer, Roger Spencer, had told me that some thought the river's course could have been as far east as Goring-by-Sea, six miles away. I'd also heard it said the old Oyster Pond near the seafront on its eastern flank was the only remnant from the river's original meanderings. Not far away from the pond, a 13-storey block of flats called Kingmere has been built on piles as high as the flats, standing in the old gravel bed of the river. Its residents say that on a windy day you can feel the building sway. It was entirely possible, Roger had said, that the old Arun had had several outlets to the sea in the days when this area had been so swampy and marshy.

Nowadays, rivers are rerouted to accommodate new development. Back in the 1730s, the river mouth had to be re-cut because the easterly currents and prevailing south-westerlies meant it was heavily prone to silting. It's thought there had to be several re-cuts in different places, as one entrance after another filled with sand and silt. Even if ships managed to negotiate the harbour mouth, they then had to navigate one or more of the winding channels in order to reach Littlehampton or sail further up the Arun.

The eventual solution was to cut an entirely new harbour channel, running straight from the old town quay, by the modern 'Look and Sea Centre', down to the sea. That's why, when you stand there on the town quay, you are really looking straight out to sea.

The work to change the river's course needed a private Act of Parliament before it could begin. Wooden piers were then built on either side of the river mouth to hold its new position and to make it easier to dredge the new harbour entrance. The modern piers you can see today are built on the lines of the 18th century ones but you can still see some of the old timbers poking out of the water on the western side at low tide.

I was on my way to the Town Quay now. I found the bell I was looking for and rang it. It was the home of a distinguished academic, who was also an emeritus professor at the University of Hong Kong. Professor Brian Morton's speciality was marine ecology and, from the research he had done, I could see it was entirely appropriate that his first name was an anagram of brain.

There again, all I really knew about him was that he wanted to turn Littlehampton golf course into a wetland reserve. Nature had been reshaped by human intervention in the 18th century. Now, the professor wanted nature to have the last laugh. Revenge is a dish best served cold and it had already been almost three centuries. The professor himself had also been an elusive quarry, but that evening he was at home to visitors in his flat in a new development in Surrey Street, overlooking the river, of course, and ready to talk about the ideas.

On first sight, Brian was a big, vigorous man and didn't look much like a pensioner – but I understood that on retiring to become emeritus professor, he'd settled down to research the story of the Arun from when, 700,000 years ago, it was just a tributary of a vast estuary, the Channel River that drained the North Sea, then the flat marshlands of Doggerland that surrounding a huge inland lake, grazed by mammoths, hippopotamuses and deer. Researching a book on the river, Brian had discovered, as had Gary Baines, that the area behind the dunes had also been marshland.

"The river used to be about three or four kilometres wide and now it's only 20 metres wide at its mouth," Brian explained, "so draining through that area of former marshland is what's locally called a rife. It works as drainage channel, but is actually a surviving tributary of the Arun. In it is a complete marsh flora and fauna."

If the golf course were to be relocated as the professor was proposing, and a chunk of the west river bank removed, the tide would reclaim its own, recreating the marshland that used to exist. He wanted to create a wetland reserve in Littlehampton. It had been done elsewhere, such as on the River Crouch in Essex, at Burnham-on-Crouch.

"I understand it's not going to be popular with the golfers. But you know, I think there are bigger considerations than just simply playing golf. This county has lost most of its wetlands." The professor sighed. He had a persuasive argument. He leaned across to offer me a dish of peanuts. Brian's daughter and her husband, a policeman, sat listening. We were in the sitting room overlooking the water. It was night and the river was out there, a mass of blackness, at one with the sky, ready and willing to play its part in the professor's plans. If anyone's the man to do it, it's the professor. There was already a marsh in Hong Kong that owed its entire recreation to him. It was a little smaller than the golf course, he said, but attracted more than 40,000 visitors a year. That was more than the number of golfers in Littlehampton, he said. He knew how he wanted his nature reserve to be; it would be 'fronted' by a beautiful set of sand dunes, with an education centre and tours.

"It would be a major tourist draw with the reserve based around a large lake, flushed by the tide. Landward, you'd walk from Rope Walk to the sand dunes, along what is almost certainly a mediaeval road." The road was one the professor had seen on old maps. "And," he added, "The fort would be a focal point on his tour. It is a national disgrace that the Napoleonic fort is covered with ivy." Brian had a conspiracy theory to explain the mystery surrounding it. He is convinced the barracks were blown up to create the number 1 hole and the tee for the number 2. Brian had published his proposals and lectured on them. There was a major obstacle, however. The golf course, which had bought the freehold from a previous Duke of Norfolk, was quite happy where it was.

6

Scorcher

I cut inland to a street of terraced houses. Scorcher had been born in one of them. Scorcher was a craggy octogenarian and local legend. His house in New Road was built when the road really was new and Littlehampton's population was only seven thousand served by five butcher shops and three fishmongers catering for the shipbuilding community of men and their families.

Scorcher's real name was Derek Goldsmith, but he carried his rebellious nickname as a badge of 'dishonour' passed down through a generation after his father was given it in 1910 for speeding in the town on a bicycle.

"They fined him five shillings for scorching up the high street." Scorcher's pride was evident. As I shook hands with Scorcher, I couldn't help but think of him as a male version of 'Miss Haversham', enthroned in his upholstered armchair, looking as if he never moved from it; except that Scorcher had wed. Beside him, Scorcher's wife, deep in her own armchair, introduced herself as Dorothy.

Scorcher's father and the first of that name had crewed for Hubert Parry when the composer farmed in Rustington. Other artists had also sailed here, like the poet Helaire Belloc, who grew up in the county and wrote about it, sailing his favourite yacht, Nona, and an old cutter called Jersey, along the coast. Surely named after the poet, is Belloc Road in Wick. Hubert Parry, meanwhile, loved to entertain on board and had the 80ft Wanderer, named for the old river, extended in the middle so it could accommodate more of his friends.

"So he could go to Ford," Scorcher explained to me looking at me levelly. I was confused. Ford wasn't on the river, only the old canal.

"The Norwegian Fjords!" Scorcher shouted as if I were hard of hearing and mad with it.

Like the Old Bugger, Scorcher had been born and bred in Littlehampton and had run bare-legged on its river banks. At 14, he too had worked at Hillyard's on the wharf. Scorcher remembered things that other people had forgotten or never knew, like a man named Bill Yates, who had been the ferryman across the Arun for some 50 years.

"All the children used to catch eels and sell them for a shilling a pound at the fisheries. We made money out of it. After we came home from school, we had our dinners, then you'd pick up a needle and repair some nets before going out to play. The families along Pier Road where the fishermen lived would have their back doors open. We could go in any of them in the winter and have a cup of soup."

As well as the river, the children had had the beach as their playground. "The West Beach was the best beach in England. Pure sand from the pier right the way through to Climping. And now it's all shingle," Scorcher muttered sternly, "caused by dredging for ballast and sand for building," He drew breath and continued. "Before the War, that old dredger, the Lord Leaconsfield, used to take 90 ton of mud out to sea more or less every day. On the banks of the wharves, there is about 10 or 12ft of mud now to what there was. On a neap tide, the boats that moor there are all high and dry. They barely touched the ground on big springs in the old days."

Scorcher had recently been put in charge of the town's river regattas, but had kicked up a rumpus when the greasy pole of his childhood had been ruled out by health and safety because of the high insurance. The old regattas had been full of rowing and sailing races and diving and swimming competitions. But the highlight was the greasy pole with a flag on the end.

"You had to walk the pole which was about 30ft long, to get the flag to win the prize of a leg of pork. All the kids did it and fell in the river! Tiger Moths from Ford Aerodrome flew overhead and bombed everyone with flour bombs!" Scorcher's face lit up and he described playing a water baby at Christmas in pantomime at the Windmill Theatre on the seafront. And he remembered travelling acts too, like Harry Joseph's Performing Troupe.

"And Doctor White Eye," Scorcher remembered. "He had a black face with a white diamond over one eye. He and his wife were all blacked up and had to go around with a harmonium on a truck and a couple of banjos all over the town."

Like so many seaside towns, as I was to find out, Littlehampton was still awash with musicians and artists. Such as Paul, who ran a local writers' group, wrote plays and played old wartime songs like *Hello Dolly* and *Run, Rabbit Run* on the piano twice a week at the old Dolphin pub in the High Street in return for a pint and a hot lunch of pie, mash and peas every Tuesday and Thursday.

From the depths of the adjacent armchair, Mrs Scorcher – Dorothy – made me jump by suddenly calling her husband by his real name: "Derek, there used to be a big roller rink here and Pierrot shows in tall hats and dinner dances in the old seafront pavilion. Mummy always used to lose me. I'd run up and go and see the Punch and Judy on the beach."

Along with the revived regatta, Scorcher was back in business running crab-catching competitions using bait bags instead of hooks, filled with bacon, squid or fish.

"They'll eat anything," Scorcher said of the crabs. "They're ravenous creatures. They'd eat you if they could!" The most he could remember anyone catching was 400 in the space of two-and-a-half hours, each and every one of them thrown back in alive after the prizes were given out.

Scorcher had regrets apart from the greasy pole. There were not many fishermen left. But not everyone had gone. His favourite walk was along New Road to the lifeboat station, on Fisherman's Quay.

"The old fishing ways are still there, people going out in little 18ft boaters, and crabbers and potters of a morning. I can still walk all along the quay and look down the river and see what's going on. That was the place all the fishermen could pull their boats up and scrub them off and clean them."

After bidding Scorcher and Mrs Scorcher goodbye, I sought out the car park where St John's Church, a wooden fisherman's church, had once stood. It was later bought and put to use as a theatre, but got burnt down. I found the old church path. Turn down into Pier Road and the path is across the road. It was one of the fires Scorcher remembered. The other was in the bandstand in Banjo Road, named for its shape, the same as the instrument. The bandstand was in the round part of the banjo, before the War. Scorcher remembered it caught fire one evening while all the firemen were on an outing and had to cut short their merriments and rush back to tackle the blaze.

7

Harbour Lights

A vast amount of silver foil, old milk bottle tops and stamps had been donated to buy the town's first ever inflatable lifeboat, the Blue Peter 1, in 1967. Bill, one of the volunteers at the lifeboat station, which I had walked to after leaving Mr and Mrs Scorcher, as I now thought of them, told me the town's first lifeboat had proudly displayed the TV programme's famous shield and galleon logo until it was pensioned off. It has since been replaced several times over.

For me, ambling along the riverside like this was bringing back childhood memories. My father had kept a small motor boat at Littlehampton, when my sister Harriet and I were young, called the *Merle Hi*. A modest 24ft cruiser with a mustard yellow hull, its name was a hybrid of our middle names. The *Merle Hi* would sometimes venture upriver, but more often than not, much to our dismay, would just bob about at the jetty as we glumly munched on cheese sandwiches. Once, on a trip out, we ran aground on a low tide at dusk and I was carried ashore by a passing rear admiral in galoshes. If only I had been 20 years older I would have enjoyed it more. But at the time, the best bit was sitting in the prow of the *Merle Hi* with my pale legs dangling over the edge, waiting for the wash of a passing boat.

Now the river and I had changed. I rarely showed my legs, though I was walking more strongly, trailing wires from my tens machine glued with its adhesive suckers to my lower back and right leg. I had even invested in larger, butterfly-shaped suckers and gel to apply to the skin against which the suckers were pressed to increase the machine's effect.

As I walked, I passed rows of apartments that gave onto the river front. From the 19th century Littlehampton's shipyards had been prolific, producing ocean-going vessels like the 600 tonne ship that had taken the Falkland Islanders their first consignment of sheep. It had been built by Harvey's of Littlehampton, with Isemonger, Ollier, Corney and Carver other big names of that century.

There had been glamour as well as labour with a cross-channel ferry run by the London, Brighton & South Coast Railway, together with the Western Railway of France, where passengers could depart Littlehampton for Honfleur in Normandy, La Havre, St Malo and Jersey. It was also billed as being the shortest route to Caen, Tours and the West and South West of France. Three steam packets had worked the passage, the Rennes, Caroline and the cheekily-named Ida, collecting passengers from the old railway wharf, just north of where the new footbridge now is. Travellers were charged by the mile with prices ranging from 11/4d for third class to 3d for first class. Most settled for the cargo hold. But the main job of the steam packets was to carry the mail. Sadly, the Channel ferry service didn't make enough money. After it was abandoned, its infrastructure found a grim new purpose in the turbulence of the First World War, for loading armaments and ammunition destined for the Western Front, with hundreds of thousands of tons of explosives passing through the town.

Now the old shipyards were more or less gone. Many people in the town had been unhappy at that but at least the riverside was opened up. You could stroll or jog along the new walkway, punctuated by stone markers inscribed with fish recipes like 'cod in cream' and 'sea cabbage'. The cabbage was no longer in plentiful supply, since foragers had picked it for the pot in the 1700s and 1800s almost into extinction.

Regardless of the sea cabbage situation, you could walk from the railway station through the town to the riverside and watch a yacht sail out – or, as I was doing then, the slow dance of a sand dredger, the *Adurni*, as it appeared to pirouette within the banks, doing the job Scorcher's Lord Leaconsfield would have done years before.

"The dredger requires a lot of skill to manoeuvre into very narrow positions," Anne Carnegie, Littlehampton's Harbour Master, observed beside me. "It's quite a sizeable vessel."

The *Adurni* continued to manoeuvre with delicate precision for its bulk. Other vessels had spread out so the tug could work unimpeded, levelling moorings, a task it performed every two years, agitating the silt into suspension so it would be carried out with the tide. The harbour is big enough to accommodate vessels up to 70 metres long at the top of spring tides. But economies of scale had meant the shipping has steadily declined and the cranes from the railway wharf had long gone. Commercial ships were getting ever larger; today, just one ship's hold will take the equivalent of more than 50 lorries or 20-tonne dumper trucks.

"Back in the 1950s, 60s and 70s, cargos of pumice, potatoes, ash and timber were all brought and unloaded here," said Anne. "People recall there'd be six or seven ships at a time."

Only one or two boats a month docked here now, with granite chippings for Sussex roads.

Where the harbour's future lay was the job of the Trust Port, set up in a 1927 Act of Parliament, with its elected board of members to act as independent commissioners. It was their task to decide if the future was in leisure, commerce, fishing – or all three.

Anne and I took a few short steps along a stretch of the walkway as if we were gracious ladies in stiff crinolines. Apart from the dredger moving between the banks as dainty as a ballerina, there was a sideshow going on right beside the walkway – a rogues' gallery of cats, crouching, on guard over their domains or basking in the neat rectangular front gardens of the flats lining the waterfront, each according to their wont. From above, seagulls wheeled and shouted down taunts.

Anne pointed across the river, with its faded atmosphere of yesteryear. "The west bank has a very different feel to the east bank. Local people really value that."

We ambled past the old winkle beach where the swans gather on the slipway up to the Look and Sea Centre with its panoramic viewing dome. Before she continued: "People still feel very close to the sea here. There's a very strong affinity between people who have their boats here, including the charter fishermen and people with leisure boats and the people who live right on the waterside. It's an entirely different experience to the beautiful old ships that used to come into the harbour. We can't stop that happening. We can't turn the clock back, but it's important to recognise where we've come from. And that we still share the same river."

Mooring and fishing rights have always been lucrative. When Bernard, the 16th Duke of Norfolk, who owned a lot of the land in Littlehampton, sold much of the estate around 1940, the only asset retained was the bed of the River Arun! The bed in question ran from the sea at the mouth of the estuary 16 miles north to Pallingham Lock at Pulborough. The Duke's family wisely retained a further 30-odd mooring rights at Arundel itself. And sensibly, they kept their grip on another riverbed, this time the bottom of the Adur from the Norfolk Bridge in Shoreham to Partridge Green. The title of both river beds predate Domesday.

Whenever I came here, I enjoyed the changing light, deep sunsets to bone-china skies. We lingered a while then climbed the stairs to Anne's office, passing posters publicising the anti-smuggling war by harbour police, Operation Kraken. It isn't so much brandy and lace, these days as people.

Back in Anne's office, we pored over a map of the harbour. There was the narrow entrance through which the Arun joins the sea. The continual action of the tidal flows scouring out the entrance has created a permanent feature out of deposits from the river, a tidal bar on which vessels can run aground if they aren't careful. The bar's size and shape is always changing, and can vary in height by as much as 3ft.

I was already impressed with Anne's knowledge of the subject she used to teach in school, geography, but she was about to go up even higher in my estimation.

"How about a visit to the Dinky Diner?" she enquired. It turned out to be the closest thing the East Beach had to a greasy spoon.

The Dinky Diner was full and all the tables upstairs were occupied. A cheerful pre-occupied bonhomie prevailed to the sound of the scraping of plates. It was easy to see why. The portions were gargantuan. People around here, myself included, seemed to make a habit of eating breakfast at lunchtime. The Diner's patrons were tucking into the largest cooked breakfasts I had ever seen: a raft of bacon rashers, a swathe of sausages, a mountain of mushrooms, with fried bread and chips on the side, meant that every square inch of the giant plates were covered.

"Everyone in Littlehampton comes here to get the best and biggest possible breakfast you could ever eat," Anne shouted over the clatter. "Fishermen eat here before going out and at lunchtime." Fishermen, mechanics, and council workers all rubbed shoulders over the plentiful toast and fried bread. Anne then ordered a single slice of toast and sat nibbling on it daintily.

The owner, who was expecting news at any moment of the safe delivery of a new grandchild, was Boyd 'Boydie' Torode, and had run the place for the last decade. Boydie brought me what Gulliver would have recognized in his travels as a Brobdingnagian-sized vegetarian breakfast, complete with a mug of builder's, sans milk, just like I liked it. As the good book says there's a time for sowing and reaping. And also for indulgence.

8

Fish ...

I had begun going to a learners' pool at the leisure centre on Littlehampton seafront, where you could walk down shallow steps. Edging for the first few times into the warm water an hour before closing when it was at its quietest, my right knee felt as heavy as a cannonball in the water. I was usually the last person to leave the slightly-grungy changing rooms as they closed at nine o'clock. I'd leave as the girls were mopping down the floors, come out of the florescent-lit foyer into the cold night air and sit on the wall on the promenade, gazing at the pinpricks of ship's lights out on the invisible horizon in the darkness. On some clear nights, since the streetlamps were confined to the pavement across the road, the only light on the seaward side was the bright, full moon, glistening on the restless dark body of water beyond the empty beach and huts.

I had acquired another physio at the Bognor Memorial Hospital called Mark, who told me that the greatest stress we can put on our knees is to walk downstairs. He got into the habit of walking backwards, carefully carrying his new baby and the habit stuck. I couldn't quite manage backwards yet so went sideways like a crab. I was thrilled with Mark – not because he told me I had what his wife termed footballer's knees, but because he was willing to risk saying I would definitely run again.

*

St Valentine's Day had arrived with a particularly mushy choice of card on all the shelves. I ignored the dizzying pink and red rows of cards in the shops. The day was ushered in with sheeting rain, leaving giant puddles on the highways and byways. Now I generally liked a good puddle as much as the next person, but at that moment in time I was grown old and grumpy, while Littlehampton's seafront greens were sodden. I avoided them as I made my way to the tearoom overlooking the sea at Harbour Park, the town's fun park, to meet Neil.

Sometimes you come to a town because you fall in love with it. Sometimes because you fall in love with someone in it. And sometimes, like Neil, you come for the fish. Here, the cod are on their way back. It's a fisherman's paradise and Neil suddenly realised that was where he wanted to be. He was working as a sales director when he had one of those life-changing moments.

"I had been sitting on the M25 for two-and-a-half hours on my way to Margate for another 20-minute appointment," he grimaced as we drank our tea in the park's tea-room. Nearby was an eight foot model of Nelson's ship H.M.S Victory and I was delighted to realise that my favourite pub grub of fish fingers, chips and peas was also on offer. "Then it was another two-and-a-half hours back to London for more meetings with more traffic jams. I thought, 'there has got to be more to life than this'."

Neil started looking for a boat and eventually found what he wanted, a 40ft sloop. After studying and qualifying with his Boatmaster's Licence, he launched his new business aboard the renamed sloop, *Spirit of Arun*, taking people leisure fishing off Littlehampton, sometimes as far as Alderney in the Channel Islands.

Over his mug of tea, he told me: "Littlehampton was very much a commercial fishing port in the past. People making their living from nets and going out in the middle of the night, fishing for herring and things like that. Whereas today people come to Littlehampton, stay in Littlehampton, eat in its restaurants and go out fishing for a hobby."

There are still 14 commercial fishing boats registered out of Littlehampton and many smaller ones worked by individuals, pairs and families netting and potting at Littlehampton. But leisure fishing is on the up.

Neil regaled me with fishing stories and I forgot about my fish fingers, chips and peas. I was surprised about some of the fish to be found off Littlehampton. Some are big. There is a type of shark distantly related to the Great White that lives in deep water that might give you a nip if you came across it, as

Neil has. There were even underwater chalk mountains off the coast here called the Kingmere Rocks, where black sea bream make their nests on its surface, so that down in the murk it looked like the cratered surface of the moon. The salt-water bream are a popular delicacy in France, where the bream is also fished. The story of the black bream off Littlehampton is a fascinating one. Thousands upon thousands come here every year to spawn between April and June. Neil swore that Littlehampton was the best place in Britain to catch black bream.

"We also get a lot of sea bass, and then in the winter months we would predominantly fish for cod and whiting."

There is another reason why some of the most plentiful fish stocks are here off the Sussex coast – the wrecks.

"There was a lot of shipping going on throughout the Second World War that was bombed and became casualties of war," Neil told me. "We've got 60 or 70 wrecks within a 35 to 40-mile radius of the port and they act as big food chains. Fish go there to breed, then bigger fish predate on smaller fish and so you get this whole eco-system around an old shipwreck."

You could dive the wrecks too. They were perfect fishing grounds for Neil to let the *Spirit of Arun* drift over. One of the best known is the *Shirala*, some five or six miles south-west of the harbour entrance. Another, a sunken bomber, one of the many wrecks off the coast, is also lying on the seabed, some two-and-a-half miles from the harbour mouth, its role transformed from a killing machine into a shelter for fish to spawn.

9

...and chips

I'd heard on the news that we now had a National Potato Day. It was fitting moment as my jigsaw journey was about to lead me down past a parade of shops that might well contain the highest number of establishments serving fish'n'chips in the county. Perhaps, like estate agents, a cluster of them attracts business. But there will always be an element of rivalry, and on Arun Parade, two hard-boiled chippies go head to head.

At that point, I was faced with a daunting choice. Osca's or Fred's? I have heard folk swear allegiance to both. My mother used to be for Osca, but has since switched allegiance to Fred; my stepfather was Fred's man, but each would happily eat in both. Fred's claims to have won the coveted title of 'National Fish and Chip Shop' on several occasions – surely quite a feat if it had.

The Fred of Fred's really did exist. At the time he was living above the eponymous chip shop, having handed it over to his son, Chris, some years before. Chris, who was helped in the chippie by his wife and daughter, brought me over a plate of fish and chips. It was time to become a connoisseur in the consideration of bouquet, texture and provenance.

"When you pick a chip up, it should bend," Chris said. "It's mainly to do with the sugar content. A darker one has too much. With a low-sugar potato you get a nice-coloured, tasty chip." Good quality fish and chips were the best takeaway food, he insisted. At Fred's, only the best chipping potatoes were used, fluffy Maris Pipers and fresh oil daily to fry them in separate to the fish, burgers and saveloys, steering clear of hydrogenated and trans fats. Size matters, too. Some chippies believe in chunky chips.

"The thinner the chip, the more fat content you get. But we need one that cooks reasonably fast – so we go for one in the middle. But people seem to love them." Chris was considering experimenting to see whether a chipped potato in its skin could prove popular.

Every morning at Fred's, the chips are fresh cut without knowing how many customers the day will bring. A chippie's forecast is only ever about 60 per cent right. Like all the other seafront businesses in Littlehampton praying for a good season, Chris was a hostage to sunshine.

"We depend on the weather through the summer. If the weather's not with us, we'll have a poor one. If we have a good summer, we're all on our knees by the end of it. Sometimes the seaside season can start early and end late, if the sun shines in February and doesn't stop until October."

I accepted all this, though I am more of a winter chip eater.

"Littlehampton is a strange place," Chris told me. "In the summer, it goes absolutely mad. But by seven o'clock, you're back to a nice village atmosphere."

He thought he had the best of both worlds in a shop like his. "Sometimes there are queues along the river road 200 yards long. It's hard to keep on top of it. People are amazingly patient waiting and everyone's really friendly. That's what makes fish and chips the best job. There aren't many jobs where you get praise from people. You can't buy that sort of thing. There's nothing that makes you feel better than someone saying, 'that's the best fish and chips I've ever had'."

The family bought the place because they wanted somewhere where you could work hard for six months and then shut down and take it easy for six – which a few of the restaurants used to do. Not so any more. Now it is fish and chips all year round. From 11.30 every morning with a two-hour break on Mondays and Thursdays, then open again until nine o'clock at night.

*

That was the first time I tried Fred's excellent chips, but not the last. After meeting Fred and his family, I would sometimes make a beeline for the chippie, often peering into the nearby window of the tiny Links View Gift Shop with its ornamental shells and lighthouses and my favourite, miniature plastic globes, each holding captive a snowy scene of a minuscule beach-hut. One time I stood against the railings on an early evening overlooking the river. It was raining but I was happy enough with a bag of chips warming my hands. It reminded me of another time and another bag of chips. I'd got off the train from a long day's work in London and starving hungry, had bought a bag of chips near my local station and gone to look for my car: only to find it had been moved because the area had since been cordoned off by the police for a football match. Remembering that night, I giggled, leaning against cold metal then swallowed another hot Maris Piper chip, the swans of the Arun congregating for nightfall in the lee of the bank below.

10

Show time

Ronnie Barker used to live on the seafront in Littlehampton's South Terrace. But the comedian got fed up with the bureaucracy when he tried to refurbish his bay windows. I soon found that although people in the town seemed to know what colour toilet Barker had when he lived in the house – pink – no one could tell me which house it was.

At the Civic Centre in Maltravers Drive, one of the archivi sts helped me go through the records of planning applications. We knew it had been sometime in the 1970s, somewhere in South Terrace.

Finally we found what we were looking for. Ronnie had lived at number 23. I found his sketch for a new bay window. There were several letters, too. I photocopied everything just before the Civic Centre closed for the day, took my treasures and headed home.

Ronnie's frustration with bureaucracy became apparent as I read his correspondence to the area planning officer, a Mr Littlefield.

Ronnie wanted permission to restore the bay windows, which he said were rotten. Infuriatingly, I found that my precious photocopy of an indignant letter from him was incomplete. It ran out on page two with the tantalising words, "it is perhaps a little unreasonable to expect me to…" Expect me to what? I rang the council and a copy of the missing page arrived promptly the next day when I read on. Ronnie argued the cost of 'a complete new handmade set of bays' would be 'exhorbitant' (sic) at perhaps £5,000 – misspelling the word with an 'h'. An official note stamped 12th August, 1976 recommended refusal, citing 'an intrinsic part of the character of the building' which was listed after the comedian bought it, to become part of the historic seafront walk. No new windows for Ronnie.

I tried to imagine Ronnie's voice, so familiar to me from wooing Nurse Gladys Emmanuel in *Open All Hours* or cajoling Fletcher in *Porridge*, having a serious conversation with a planning officer and failed.

It was a blustery day with an angry sea glimpsed beyond the greens as I walked along South Terrace to stop outside No 23. Ronnie's old house was at least five storeys high, with four steps leading up to the front door and possibly an attic. It was difficult to be sure from my worm's eye view on the pavement in front of the building.

Just round the corner in Norfolk Road was a little café with salmon pink window frames, where I paused for a moment to read the menu which included a fishermen's breakfast of kippers and scrambled egg, as well as intriguingly, Christmas pudding and cream. Next door the cafe was a general store with post office and off-licence that had apparently inspired Ronnie to write *Open All Hours*. I bought a paper and, whistling, strolled from Norfolk Road into Granville Road. G-G-Granville! So that was where the name for David Jason's character in *Open All Hours* came from.

*

Due west from the former Barker residence with its once questionable bay windows was a guest house called Racing Greens, which Alan Thomas and his wife, Eileen, had bought when they retired. At the age of nine, Alan had been brought to Littlehampton for a family holiday and he had never forgotten it.

He was on guest house duty cooking English breakfasts in an upstairs kitchen when I stopped by to say hello. The town doesn't have a big hotel like it used to in its halcyon days but there were a lot of guest houses and I wanted to meet someone who ran one of them. Watching Alan, it occurred to me that scrambled eggs occupied almost as prominent a position in my travel itinerary round Littlehampton as fish and chips.

"I was at that age when you're just a bit too young to kiss a girl." Alan stirred the scrambled egg with a wooden spoon.

The town had left an impression on several others who had passed through, like the comedian Paul O'Grady who, like Alan, went on seafront rides while he was living in Littlehampton. As a young man in the 1970s, before he hit the drag-queen circuit and made his name as Lily Savage, Paul sold ice creams on the seafront. In a chapter about Littlehampton in his autobiography The Devil Rides Out, Paul sounds restless and lonely. Until his friend 'Vera' arrives. After that, life blossoms into one long holiday with carnival parades, getting soaked on speed boats and breathless rides on the rollercoaster that was the Wild Mouse.

Unlike Paul, more than 50 years later, Alan had returned to Littlehampton: The breakfast dishes were ready. "If I had kissed a girl," he said, "I'd have probably got a clip round the ear from my mother."

*

Victorian Littlehampton had more than 40 respectable boarding houses offering lodgings. The town was a sort of summer camp for posh nannies and their charges, more genteel and respectable and suitable for children than Brighton, famous for its dirty weekend. Old photos of Littlehampton show nannies in their primly starched caps and uniforms pushing perambulators on the prom, while donkeys from the nearby village of Wick took children for rides along the sands. Less than a mile, but another world away on the wharves, the town's lifeblood was being pumped by the ship-building and fishing industries, with the local abundant supply of cod, whiting and herring. But boom time as a family holiday destination for working class families was just around the corner. Billy Butlin's arrival after the Great

Depression in the 1930s turned Littlehampton into a day tripper's paradise. The charabancs came in their hundreds. Families and couples came to take a dip, sniff the sea air and eat a picnic of bread, jam and margarine polished off with an ice cream from one of the local vendors, Uncle Charlie, Uncle George and Uncle Tony, who not only sold ice creams but put on puppet shows. By 1934, the town had grown so popular the council held a meeting on whether to ban visitors. But it was decided everyone had a right to the beach and the motion was rejected.

*

I was walking the next leg of my journey with a man whose charmed childhood had included swimming in the sea with elephants and whose day job had been to put his head inside the jaws of a killer whale called Ramu: my third Gary, Gary Smart, scion of the circus dynasty, now owned the fun park having bought it in the 1970s from the Rank Organisation, which had owned Butlin's.

I knew a little about Gary. He'd grown up in his grandfather's circus, Billy Smart's famous Big Top, and worked at the family's animal safari parks where he'd look after Ramu. It turned out that Ramu had also looked after Gary. One day, the 22ft whale bumped into him in the pool, cracking two ribs. Realising he'd hurt his human friend, the whale stopped dead so Gary could hold onto his dorsal fin. Then Ramu took him to the side of the pool and rolled him gently to safety out of the water.

I stirred my coffee. It was no hardship to be sitting here waiting in the fresh sea air. A vocal punch-your-weight machine articulated itself every so often behind me. Further off, a carousel whirled, spinning painted ponies, laughter and the kind of magic that only whirligigs and circuses can weave in the buttercup sunshine.

It wasn't the first time I'd been here. Like Alan, I had come as a child, after a day of bobbing on the *Merle Hi*. I vividly remembered walking barefoot through the amusement arcade that had seemed vast to me back then, then through to the beach beyond and the luxuriant feel of the soft, sun-warmed sand beneath my toes.

I'd been told Gary sat enthroned at a huge golden desk in his upstairs office with a photo of Elvis Presley on the wall and thought we probably wouldn't get on. He had sounded like he didn't suffer fools gladly on the phone when I rung asking to meet him as I walked through the town.

Gary appeared balancing a china cup and saucer, which he set down opposite mine on the picnic table. He'd soon launched into a story about the fun park's history and his own circus past. I was surprised. Instead of an irascible megalomaniac, he was cheerful and down-to-earth.

"It all started with my grandfather's coconut shy," he said. "During the Second World War, Granddad – who everyone knew as the Guv'nor – built up a travelling funfair. It went all over London. His customers were the American GIs. That's where he made his money."

Then one day, Gary explained, just after the War when the GIs had gone home, Billy Smart went out for a Sunday drive where he chanced upon a circus, and bought the whole thing outright. "He said to my Dad, you better go down the road,

I've just bought a circus. My Mum was the trapeze artiste there and that's how they met."

Punctuated by the occasional shriek from the rides, Gary told me about his childhood. His father, Ron, was one of 10 and Gary had 25 cousins at the circus. Everyone had their own jobs to do.

"I had a Shetland pony to groom. They were all named after drinks. Mine was called Sling. And Sling had to be perfectly groomed, or else. You had a sort of metal scrubbing brush to remove dead skin from cleaning the animal that left an imprint on a board behind. There was a stable master who checked the number of imprints. If there weren't enough and you hadn't groomed it properly, you were in trouble. You learned to look after animals at a very young age."

Gary used to swim with the circus elephants in the sea off Southsea, Morecambe and Swansea Bay, sitting high on an accommodating back as the animal plodded across the road, down the beach and into the water to cool off.

"Health and safety wouldn't allow you to do that now, let alone walk about 20 elephants through town to the train station when we were moving on," said Gary. I thought of Scorcher's flower-bombing and greasy pole. "But the elephants were always very gentle with us children. In the sea we would dive off them and they were so careful not to hit us or tread on us."

When the circus troupe arrived in a place, the whole town turned out and followed the parade, throwing pennies at the visitors. In the early days Billy Smart's often entertained the post-war crowds on bomb sites like Emerald Street in Leicester. The circus was a magical thing that delivered a panacea for the hardships and privations of the war years.

"Didn't your schooling suffer though?" I asked.

"I have an attendance card from when I was five. I went to 20 schools from Scotland down to Cornwall. There were bullies who were jealous and girls who were curious. But we always had plenty to eat and it was always warm and dry. What more could you want?"

As Gary grew up, he realised he preferred the operational side to performing in the ring. "I was better behind the scenes, getting things ready on time and keeping a 5,000-seater tent up in a Gale force 8. The crowd don't see it when it's like First World War mud and you've got to haul everything in, winch the trucks out, move a hundred miles, be up all night to put the tent up again and then put on the paint and sequinned costumes." He wagged a finger. "But hard work never hurt anyone."

Years later, Gary was working with another animal handler and a tiger nearly escaped over a wall. "I shouted at him to pull the tiger down again by the tail." Somehow they all survived.

Billy Smart's circus never came to Littlehampton, only pitching in the bigger towns of Bognor and Worthing. But one day, like his grandfather had chanced upon the circus 30 years earlier, Gary and his father found themselves in Littlehampton.

"We sat down on the wall and had our fish and chips and it looked all nice and busy. My father Ron said the fun park was a nice little business. Very seasonal. It's not a huge fun park. You haven't got enormous overheads. You can pull down the shutters at the end of the season, go away for the winter, then come back and start over."

Gary picked up our coffee cups and whistled for his dog, Ruby, a black Labrador. Ruby showed she could pull a trick with a chocolate biscuit. When one was thrown to her, she caught it on her nose then hoovered it up in a trice. After the biscuit performance, we set off for a tour of the seafront 'Kingdom of Fun' turning round at Fisherman's Hard, the slipway by the Town Quay, during which I learned Gary had been in the Territorial Army. His ancestral relative, William Smart, had fought at the Battle of Trafalgar. At the fun park, Gary pointed out the old miller's wheel from the windmill that had stood where the Windmill Theatre was, where Scorcher had made his debut in The Water-Babies. There were layers of history, even in a fun park. Giant toy soldiers, rescued from Butlin's buildings in the old holiday camps, stood guard at the park walls, their flags cracking smartly in the sea breeze, right by the earlier garrison fort now holding up a crazy golf course.

"You have to be careful – not too tacky and not too sterile," was Gary's advice.

We walked a circuit around the 'Kingdom of Fun' perimeter, blending with others buying ice cream, doughnuts and chips out on the promenade, along the wooden pier, down Pier Road, then back towards the Oyster Pond. Some said the pond, perhaps a remnant of the old Arun, had been used for keeping oysters fresh in the days when there were local oyster beds here, then for paddling and ice-skating in cold winters. On a day in the future, Gary and I would work together to put on a display of model boats on the same Oyster Pond, with the help of a group of enthusiasts called the Surface Warships Association. On that day, a bold flotilla of miniature warships took to the pond under wild, windy and wet skies, with the enthusiasts warning us that for the models, the unruly, ruffled waters of the pond were the equivalent to navigating in Gale force 8 for a real ship. In the event, only one of the models went turtle and the boats were filmed for the local BBC news. But at that moment, the only thing in the pond was a dog, a black Labrador that looked suspiciously like Gary's pet Ruby, enjoying a dip.

*

Having put down the tentative roots of the convalescent, who realises they have already stayed on longer than originally intended, I had also started singing again. The catalyst was a musician who was a former taxi driver in Littlehampton, called John Gradwell. I called him by the acronym of his initials to distinguish him from all the Johns who even outnumbered the Garys. Now in his 70s, Jah had reinvented himself as a gigging jazz musician, giving lectures about jazz greats like Dizzy Gillespie, Dave Brubeck and Anita O'Day at the University of the Third Age. Jah played guitar, banjo, mandolin and piano. Together we rehearsed some of the old standards.

Years before, travelling through the Greek islands as a student, I hadn't sung for my supper, but for my breakfast. A taverna on the island of Symi just off its larger sister, Rhodes, had paid me each morning with a boiled egg, an orange that I would solicitously peel, and a café metrio Helleniko (moderately sweet, thick Greek coffee). To earn it, I sang Crystal Gale's *Don't It Make My Brown Eyes Blue* and New Seeker songs to the accompaniment of guitar chords to diners the night before. Now as Jah and I practised together, Kitty the rescue cat would lie on the sheet music clearly enjoying the buzz of activity around her and the contribution she was making with her presence.

Jah came from a musical family. His father had worked the cruise ships as a drummer, his mother taught piano and his sister had been a contortionist in a tap dancing trio. As a child, he'd earned pocket money with another job in Littlehampton, involving neither the hackney cab nor the musical note, but mice.

"My mother had a friend who was a conjurer and ran Mouse Town in Butlin's. He gave me a part-time job."

"Tell me more," I commanded, as the cat pricked up an ear, putting down the song sheet with the words for Cry Me a River. The conjurer and Mouse Town were entirely consistent with his family history.

"I would catch a bus to the Spotted Cow. I had to walk through the arcade and down St Catherine's Road and into the Mouse Town every Saturday and Sunday. It was my job to clean and feed the mice and make sure they were in town when visitors turned up expecting a show." Thus it was at the age of 12 that Jah had 150 mice under his stewardship, males and females all in together, black, white and piebald.

"We had to wake them up when people came. I used to dress up in a gorilla suit and go on the bumper cars and everyone would follow me back into the Mouse Town. I used to get 1/6 a day (one shilling & sixpence). I had a fabulous time working there. I used to look forward to it. My first task was to open up the back of Mouse Town. You'd put your hand into this big pile of mice, pick them up and move them onto the 'town'. They all lived in a corner. When you put them on the roof of their 'town', the first thing they did was run back to their corner. They hated the 'town' really; it was just a front."

The cat laid her ear down again and shifted on her manuscript mat, none the wiser as to the content of our conversation. Kitty understood the language of music better. Littlehampton's Mouse Town – if only she knew! The 'town' itself later relocated to Bognor Pier, Jah said, but it wasn't nearly as good as Littlehampton's. Well, he would, wouldn't he?

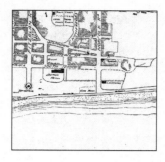

11

Beachbums and buried treasure

It was still a bit too early in the year for sunbathers. The row of brightly-painted beach huts was shut. Walking along what everyone here called East Beach was quite different to being on West Beach. Both stirred the soul with their open horizons. But on East Beach you felt connected to life in the town, unlike the more remote shore where the cormorant and the yellow-horned poppy ruled as king and queen. The promenade was always astir – even out of season. I was walking east from the Kingdom of Fun at the fun park. There were dog walkers, skateboarders, grannies with babies in buggies. Visitors came too. Sea baptisms were carried out here with the initiate clad in white robes for the ceremony. A short while ago I had struck up a conversation with a French unicyclist on his daily trip up and down the prom alongside the seafront greens.

I still couldn't jog or run yet, but was becoming more daring on my feet. When the tide was far out, I could now pick my way over the slimy clumps and humps of seaweed-clad rocks and pebbles, which go perhaps a third of a mile out on a spring tide, to stand at the water's edge.

It was a little before sundown and I saw a lone man with a metal detector. The beachcomber was patiently moving it from side to side over the sands.

"Hello!" I called.

His silhouette was outlined against the setting sun, a bit like a werewolf backlit against the full moon. Daniel, it transpired, was someone you'd see on the beach at the end of most days in and out of season. Like the werewolf, he was a member of an often despised and ostracised race and a scavenger of carrion. Except Daniel and his kind picked over pebbles instead of bones. Daniel was a treasure hunter who used a metal detector.

Daniel reluctantly paused in his labours, turned off his machine and came and spoke to me as I tried to engage him in conversation. He was another émigré from London, a former lighting engineer, who'd fled the turbulence and tantrums of a backstage job of Covent Garden to seek peace and tranquillity detecting on the sands for buried treasure.

Like a shopper who knows where to get his favourite groceries at the best price, Daniel knew the right beaches to go for a particular kind of treasure. "Bognor is good for finding money. Brighton and Worthing are good for jewellery. But there's heavy competition." On Littlehampton beach, he has more of a clear field.

Hoards are often found through the haphazard turn of a plough in a field. I'd read that a man who'd recently uncovered an Anglo Saxon hoard worth millions with his metal detector had credited the spirits of the place for his sensational good fortune, rather than blind chance or science. Daniel's method was simply to recover the treasure at the best time of low tide.

Incredibly, Daniel said he made enough from what he found on the beach to live on: £1 coins, modern rings and, once, a diamond ring. But his greatest discovery was a gold ring that he swore was the twin of one ring in Littlehampton Museum, from the wreck of the *Shirala*.

"It was a signet ring from a sailor. It must have come off the body of a sailor that drowned on the wreck."

Daniel held out his hands. They were decorated with rings like one of those ring trees that keep your jewellery tidy, all of which he said he had found on the beach. He was also wearing a 49 gram nine-carat gold chain and a watch valued at £450 and had a Samsung mobile phone which he had found in its case. The total value, Daniel said, was around £2,000, all harvested from Littlehampton beach. As well as the fabled Shirala ring, he had found a William of Orange coin minted in 1696 and a 24 carat gold French ring with the Napoleonic crest.

I noted down Daniel's astonishing annual yield. About 60 rings a year, more than one a week. The previous year, he had turned up 13 gold and six silver rings including part of a hoard. I would have to find myself a metal detector and have a go myself. Or more precisely, I would have to find someone who had a metal detector and have a go myself.

*

People told me Tyndall Jones owned a metal detector. Tyndall was well-known in the town. His family had had a shop at the top of the High Street. It was one of those old-fashioned sports shops. The door pinged as I pushed it inwards. Its interior was dark wood with shadowy recesses that smelt of leather, stacked with shoeboxes of Nike and Adidas, lit by florescent running shoes. Tyndall had sold the family shop, but still liked to help out occasionally and was serving a customer when I went in as had been arranged.

A sales assistant took over and Tyndall and I set off with his gear along the route taken by the Littlehampton Bonfire Society procession every year. The Bonfire Society, which Tyndall had been a member of for more than 40 years, was an important charity in the town. It had lit an annual bonfire on the seafront since 1952.

The procession always begins at the Maltravers Social Club, then continues onto Granville Road, St Winifred's Road, Church Street, Beach Road, St Catherine's Road and South Terrace, with the fireworks and bonfire on East Beach Green. Out of deference to the Catholic Dukes of Norfolk, the Society didn't burn an effigy of the Pope like some other bonfire marches I'd been to and for many years had held the record for raising the most money for charity. I promised myself I'd walk the procession in October, when up to 40,000 people come to watch the celebrations with the marching bands and floats and see the bonfire lit on the beach. But that afternoon, it was a procession of two, as Tyndall's and my reflection, carrying our equipment, slid by in the office window of the *Littlehampton Gazette*.

"I had an old aunt – Auntie Jessie – who was slightly eccentric," Tyndall explained, pausing to switch on the detector, letting it hover over the shingle once we were on the beach. We had a small, sturdy, metal spade, ready to dig if we got a signal. "When I was a boy, Aunt Jessie took me beachcombing after high tide and it instilled in me a love of finding things. If you do beach detecting all the time, you get a feel for it."

Evening was the best time, he said. There were fewer people around and it was less embarrassing: "It can look as if you're waiting for them to drop coins."

I told him about Daniel's claim to make a living from his metal-detecting. Tyndall quite believed it and his ears pricked up when he heard about the rings. "If he got a very old one, then he was very, very lucky, very privileged. You do get rings on the beach. Swimmers lose rings." He had heard too of Roman coins being found on West and East Beach; people dropped things sheltering in the lee of the groynes. I was hoping for some precious remnant of the past, that had patiently waited out the centuries for us, but Tyndall cautioned that our haul was more likely to be ring pulls and bottle tops.

I remembered that people often say you always find the best shells after a storm where the sea bed had been shaken up. In the unlikely event that we found treasure we would be entitled to half. The laws of Treasure Trove meant two or more gold or silver coins or 10 bronze constituted a hoard of treasure. If a museum then wants to buy what you have found, you get half, as does the landowner, which might be the crown on public land like a beach. There's a catch if it is below the low tide mark though, with any find below that point needing to be reported to a very grand-sounding official called the Receiver of Wreck.

I trotted out the story of lucky Terry Herbert, the man who said he had been led by spirits to the spot on farmland in Staffordshire and told to dig for the largest gold and silver hoard ever found, that turned out to be worth a seven figure sum.

"Hmm," sighed Tyndall. "Well, if I see a weird bump in the ground, I want to know what's underneath."

He has found Bronze Age arrow heads, belt buckles, seal matrices, a gold coin and a 17th century children's gold ring that had gone to Littlehampton Museum. Traces of black enamel and the style of the ring had helped historians at the British Museum to date it. Tyndall liked to detect on the beaches in the summer when he couldn't get out on the fields hidden under their crops. Sometimes he went treasure-hunting by the river mouth where he'd found lead musket balls. He was also a Good Samaritan and had more than once been called urgently into action to find a lost ring. One he had salvaged was the Deputy Town Clerk's engagement ring!

"Another time the editor of the *Gazette* dropped his wedding ring!" Tyndall laughed. "He was doing an interview in a field of bullocks and the animals started being inquisitive. He tried to push them away and the ring slipped off his finger and was trodden into the mud somewhere."

They had to abandon their first attempt at finding the ring when the bullocks advanced again. It was only after the farmer moved his animals into another field that Tyndall was able to search in safety and Roger's ring was rescued.

But Tyndall reminded me that not everyone loves a metal detective. "There's some called night hawkers. They do it without permission. They go at night using headlamps. They are basically grave-robbing. It's a criminal offence and they should be prosecuted. They are an absolute curse and give us all a bad name."

We crunched across the shingle together to where the loose gravel met the sand. The tide was out, the wind cool and salty.

Suddenly there was a chirp, a signal from the detector. We had found something. Was it a Roman coin or a modern penny? It was neither, just scrap metal.

Other false alarms followed, but eventually we struck lucky. It wasn't treasure from a sunken fleet, just a humble £1 coin where the nickel brass had gone green. There was another bleep. Probably just the wet sand, said Tyndall, which could create an unstable signal. As he dug down, he held the detector over the freshly-troweled loose sand. We got another faint bleep.

"Means whatever's down there is either buried treasure or a shallow ring-pull," he grinned. Sure enough it was our first ring pull. Next we dug up what might have been part of a Second World War bullet. We were on a roll.

Afterwards, we did some beach housekeeping, filling the holes in again to stop people falling in them and to leave things as we'd found them. We clambered up the shingle, a perfect red disc sinking behind the sand dunes where the Napoleonic fort was as buried as any treasure.

We turned up Fitzalan Road where the Bonfire Society's 'princess' would be transported on her 'royal' float when the bands marched back up after the fireworks to the social club later in the year. It felt like we had walked a long way. We hadn't, but Tyndall agreed. Despite the fact we'd been moving about, we were chilled. In the cheap pair of black woollen gloves I'd bought in Worthing Market, my fingers felt like they were dropping off. Back in the warm above the sports shop, Tyndall revived us with a pot of Earl Grey tea and a plate on which an impressive assortment of chocolate and shortbread biscuits were laid out in a fan shape. I ate them while he cleaned up what we hoped was the antique bullet – but wasn't. At least we were £1 richer from the coin we unearthed. That buffed up nicely. Hunting for buried treasure had put me in fine fettle, ready to confront my next piece of the jigsaw.

12

The medium, the witch and Knucker

The treasures on display on little shelves near the fireplace in the Dolphin, one of Littlehampton's oldest pubs, had also come from the sea, White Star ephemera from the shipping company that owned the doomed Titanic and her more fortunate sister ship Olympic, a liner that ended up as scrap.

I was seated beside the small hearth sipping from a mug of coffee and typing up my notes. The evenings were still chilly and the barman had just added fresh anthracite to the flickering logs. I wondered whether to give the barely smouldering fire a poke, when suddenly it caught. It was the end of the football season and everyone else in the pub seemed to be focused on the Man U match on a screen the size of a small cinema at the far end of the bar. Yet this wasn't your typical watering hole. There was more than just the habitual football vibes here.

The Dolphin has a history distinguished from playing host to some of our most illustrious romantic poets. The mad, bad and dangerous-to-know Lord Byron had been a guest when he was a young sprig of 17 and nearly drowned near the harbour on a mad, bad and dangerous swim one cold winter's day in 1805 – the year Gary Smart's ancestral relative, William Smart, fought in that famous sea battle at Trafalgar. Samuel Taylor Coleridge had also been a guest.

Coleridge was beset by anxiety attacks, doubtless exacerbated by his addiction to opium, and came seeking peace and seclusion in Littlehampton. The 19th century equivalent of scribbling on a beermat saw Coleridge use a piece of seaweed to break writer's block and return to writing verse during his seaside break. *Fancy in the Clouds: A Marine Sonnet, Little Hampton*, was his first sonnet in more than a decade and was sold nearly 200 years later to a private buyer at auction in Christie's for £7,768 – which had put it out of reach of Littlehampton's modest town museum.

There was a sudden roar and I was jerked back to the present. On a huge screen at the far end of the bar, Wayne Rooney had missed an open goal. Should have scored, I muttered, louder than I thought, as I was wearing headphones. A man at the bar turned round and looked at me. I had uttered a faux pas. The people here were supporting the local team and didn't want Rooney and United to score.

When I'd arrived at the Dolphin that morning, I'd learned that the pub's owners, Ellie and Katie, had been the first gay couple to tie the knot in a civil ceremony in the town. I was also told there were as many ghosts in the pub as there are live customers. In keeping with that, a 'pillywiggin' was in progress. That meant broomsticks and dried herbs on sale among Ellie and Katie's wartime booty of gas masks and tin helmets. I'd been drawn to a kitsch-but-strangely-charismatic cauldron, decorated with skulls and hissing smoke, that I thought could be a nice touch at dinner parties. There were books on hauntings, baskets of dried burdock for protection from psychic attack and sweet-smelling marigold flowers to give you confidence.

Under the window, two white toy poodles were curled up in their basket, chewing contentedly on what turned out to be a pig's ear. The poodles wrestled with their grisly treat under the watchful eye of Elaine, who was herself tucking into a roast dinner, while presiding over the pillywiggin.

*

Elaine had been a nurse but was now a medium. The former nurse was of an age to have been brought up by 'Victorian grandparents', both of whom were clairvoyants, so talking to ghosts seemed natural.

"I got used to them talking to nobody, though to me there was somebody," she said. "The Sunday afternoon table was always cleared for the séance."

"Have we got company at the moment? I asked.

"The children are watching," she replied. In the past I'd interviewed, among others, a ghostbuster hired by his local council to banish unwanted paranormal interference in a high rise block in Kent, a famous psychic and an Anglican bishop who performed exorcisms, so Elaine's words didn't seem particularly out of place. I remarked that the dogs didn't seem bothered.

"Oh, they're used to it," she said. "Some of it is repetition or ghostly replays like a woman taking the children to school. Some want to make contact. Sometimes it's very sad."

Elaine's friend Brenda was also helping with the pillywiggin. Brenda said she was a white witch called a hedge witch. She soon explained what that was. A hedge witch worked solo rather than in a coven. At the Autumn Equinox, while schoolchildren prepare their basket of fruit for the harvest festival, hedge witches like Brenda make soup to offer as a gift. Brenda also buried fruit.

"But I don't cast spells. I just mix herbs to make potions."

She ordered herbs from special witchy websites. "Though it's much better if you can grow your own, because there's more power in them."

She didn't always stick to the recipe. "I just look at what I've got and one or two of the herbs will jump out at you. They talk to you, they'll tell you which ones to use. I pop them in a little bowl. You keep running them through your hands so they keep picking up your energies, telling them all the time what your intentions are, what you want them to do and put them in a little sachet. I don't do anything bad. It would come back on you three times."

She mixes love powders to sprinkle a little magic on the bedroom sheets. "But," she warned sagely, "you can't force somebody to love you."

The essence of her love potion is cornflower. She might add rose petals and lavender with rose or lavender oil and a dash of patchouli for luck. The rest she wouldn't say. Brenda also hugged trees, which was powerful, but it wasn't always practical because of the dog-walkers. Queen Street in Littlehampton, she said, ran across ley lines and was a potent place.

Then she asked me: "have you been to the Knucker Hole? And that was the first time I heard of Knucker the dragon.

"It's a very eerie area, a big pond at the back of the church, all fenced off and the water is a very strange colour, very green and murky," Brenda explained. "It's a strange but magical area. Local legend had it that the dragon lived in the pond that was supposedly bottomless."

"Do you believe in the dragon?" I asked the hedge witch.

"Oh yes. He would have gone on to Arundel because it would have been all farmland. He would have been having your sheep and your cows."

*

I thought about Brenda's words as I warmed my hands at the hearth. The fire had sunk right down again. The football match was still on the screen. I clicked to save my evening notes on the recently-acquired second-hand laptop I was using for the first time. Curiously, instead of a clock or hour-glass, a little dragon appeared.

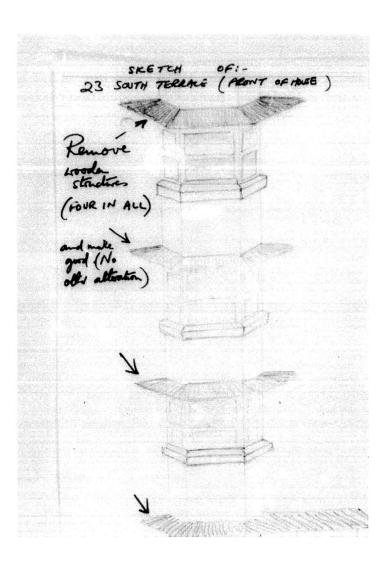

SKETCH OF:-
23 SOUTH TERRACE (FRONT OF HOUSE)

Remove wooden structures (FOUR IN ALL)

and make good (No other alteration)

Ronnie Barker sketch and correspondence (see over)

12 . 7. 76

Dear Sir -
    I enclose completed
applications for listed building
consent, and Building Regulations
forms, duly completed.

In conversation with your Mr Greenwood,
I was informed that a rough sketch of
the canopies was all that was
required in the way of drawings in
this case; this I also enclose. I
hope to hear from you soon -

          Yours faithfully,

          Ronnie B.

Pte John Barnes,
shot at dawn in 1917, and posthumously pardoned

3/

became nervous and left the tank, moving towards ARRAS where I slept the night. The next day I went on until I came to ABBEVILLE and here I asked my way to ARRAS of the Military Police. They directed me but I lost my way and was eventually arrested in BERNE.

of Witness for Prosecution recalled.

By Court Q1   What happened to your Bn. after leaving BROWN LINE trenches at 1.15 a.m. on May 3.0?

A1   We moved up to RIFLE TRENCH (front line), and at 12 Noon the same day attacked and captured SCABBARD Trench.

Character   Capt. G. Nagle Royal Sussex Rgt. sworn states:-
I produce certified true copy of A.F. B122. (attached)

Harold Peplow Major
Pres. F.G.C.M.

Extract of court–martial testimony of Pte John Barnes

Littlehampton Pier in the days before health and safety and railings c1905

Promenading on Littlehampton 'Parade' & Common, c1910

The original go-karts - goat carts with donkeys too! c1905

Prevailing westerly winds that once turned the sails of the old windmill help children's model boats along on the Oyster Pond

The Windmill in its incarnation as a casino, Beach Green, c1920

The ship 'Stralsund' entering Littlehampton Harbour, c.1920s. The decks of the ship are piled high with its cargo of timber

Man, possibly postman,
outside the Steam Packet Tavern, c1910

13

Be There Dragons?

I'd begun to collect scraps of Knucker information, learning that the local Lyminster Primary School had its school motto based around the word DRAGON. They were fine words.

D is for Dream
R is for Remember we are all different
A is for Achieve our best
G is for Grow, care and love one another
O is for Open our eyes to new ways of thinking
N is for Never give up trying.

Knucker was also the inspiration for the school crest on the pupils' blazers. I stuck up an Ordnance Survey map sent by a friend on a pinboard in my mother's garden room to see exactly where the Knucker Hole was, as if I were planning a military campaign. Knucker's Pool was in Lyminster, north of Littlehampton, beyond Wick, that had itself once been a separate village, but was now absorbed by a kind of centrifugal force into an outlying layer of the town.

Research into Knucker on the net revealed he wasn't doing such good business as Nessie, of course, or the puma that roamed Dartmoor, or even a lynx that had once been sighted in what a DJ I had once worked with called 'the back of Brighton' on the outskirts of the city heading into the open country of the South Downs. The reference library yielded more. It was a wet morning so I settled down in a corner to read through the legends and make some notes.

Knucker's name originated from the Old Anglo-Saxon word for a water-monster, Nicor. The dragon was a link between the present to the days after the fall of Rome when the Saxons first arrived, bringing their language and storytelling. Their epic poem Beowulf included references to Nicoras. One little book* quoted an earlier Dictionary of Sussex Dialect in saying that from Lyminster to Lancing, Worthing to Shoreham, the county was peppered with Nuckar or Knucker Holes. They were springs rising in the flatlands of the Downs that villagers had believed to be bottomless. The water was cold in summer, but never froze; in a frost, the water gave off a vapour, being warmer than the air.

The water in the Knucker Holes was the most vivid colour blue or a weird murky green. Every reference I came across talked about the strange colour of the water.

* *quote from 'Folklore of Sussex'*

At school, I'd been fascinated by a teacher telling us that in old folklore, dragons were always believed to guard buried treasure. The Old English word for dragon is 'wyrm'. Places with something similar in their name, like Worm Hill (of which they are many in Britain), maybe even Worms Lane in Bognor, three miles along the coast, really might, once upon a time, have had treasure in them. The names and the folk stories grew up around the rumours of money or valuables buried hurriedly by those fleeing invaders; they would have had to hide treasure they couldn't carry with them, but hoped to return to collect one day.

Settling again in my chair, I read through some of the Knucker legends. In one, the Mayor of Arundel – at a time when there had been no Littlehampton – had been instrumental in the slaying of the beast. The mayor had offered a reward to get rid of the troublesome dragon. A local farmer's boy called Jim Pulk or Puttock came up with cooking an enormous poisoned pie which he transported to the Knucker Hole in his cart. The dragon took the bait and ate the pie, then the horse and cart for good measure. Jim alone survived and cut off old Knucker's head. Another version of the story had Jim poisoned too by the pie. In a third variation, a knight won the hand of the mayor's daughter after besting the beast, which explained why there was apparently a memorial stone inscribed to the Slayer's Slab, at the parish church of St Mary Magdalene in Lyminster.

To get down to business with my dragon hunting, I needed permission to access its ancient lair, the pool which was now on private land. After googling 'fisheries in Lyminster', I struck lucky on my second call when I found myself talking to Malcolm Penn of Back Arun fisheries. Malcolm knew all about Knucker.

"You know it's bottomless there?" his tinny voice queried down the phone. "When I was working there I saw a whole tree dropped in once by the gamekeeper's father."

Was he trying to scare me in traditional fashion, I wondered? "Right," I said, "It's only supposed to be 30ft deep, but according to legend they tied six church bell ropes end to end that still didn't hit the bottom." I'd done my research.

Malcolm replied, "Up at Angmering, in Decoy Woods, there's a hole there too and that and the Knucker Hole are joined by an underground river. There's a lot of water around. The Black Ditch never runs dry either." I had no idea where that was and didn't want to interrupt Malcolm's flow. The fisheries, it turned out, were now a bird sanctuary protected by barbed wire. Malcolm had said the man who owned it lived in the third cottage on the right near the church.

"Speak to Terry Torode." Any relation to the chap from the Dinky Diner? "He's looked after the woods for 50 years," said Malcolm. He'd given me just one piece of advice. "He'll help you as long as you don't upset his ducks." I made a mental note not to upset the ducks.

I couldn't get hold of the man who lived in the third cottage on the right or the game keeper Terry Torode. After various calls, including one to the new vicar at St Mary Magdalene, I was given the name of a man called George, who'd worked for many years in the area as a farmhand. George Carmen, the vicar told me, could provide full details about Knucker.

I set off in my old but cherished little Punto, one wild, dark and windy night to find George Carmen's bungalow.

George's bungalow was, I soon found, on a road that was like an Escher painting. You were never quite sure where you were in it. And neither was I with George Carmen, because I had scarcely put a foot across the threshold when he piped up: "Don't believe in 'im m'dear," meaning Knucker. I was given a cup of tea and shown photos of the grandchildren. Then we got to the subject of the dragon. Watercress had grown in the pool, George recalled.

But then, as I was leaving, George said, "That pool was always a queer translucent colour. Blue as forget-me-nots. And we never did find out what happened to them cows."

*

In the midst of tracking an ancient mythological beast to the far flung north of Littlehampton, I came across a bird indigenous to the tropics, a chicken. The hen in question, named Nana Chicken, lived in the attic of number 44, Pier Road, with Alan John McKay in his riverside house, with a painting of a naked woman looking through the curtain in an upstairs window.

I would never have learned of the chicken's existence had I not spotted Alan. I noticed Alan because he had a 3ft radio-controlled biplane strapped to the roof of his car parked in front of the chippies on the river front. He was standing eating an ice-cream in inclement weather dressed in an aviator's hat and goggles like Biggles. Littlehampton has many wonderful eccentrics in its midst and Alan was out in pole position.

Nana, his Rhode Island Red, accompanies him not just to his favourite watering holes, including the posh Norfolk

Hotel in Arundel, but to his bank. Nana Chicken also dined out with Alan at cafes and perhaps most bizarre of all, pecked around while he was in the dentist's chair. At least Nana was house-trained. Alan explained the chicken had belonged to his daughter and had moved in with him after his offspring split from her boyfriend. I was intrigued that it was the chicken and not the daughter that had moved in with the father after the ending of a relationship. Each night after supper in the third-floor kitchen, Nana saw herself to bed, climbing four floors to her airy roost in the rafters.

*

In temporarily losing a dragon but gaining a chicken, I decided to put my dragon quest on ice. I didn't know then that it would be in the deep mid-winter that I would finally put the legend of Knucker to the test. The fact was, I was keen to get on. Time was passing and I wanted to complete uncharted jigsaw territory in the town centre. I walked away from the henhouse in Pier Road and down Surrey Street, where officers from the nearby airbase at Ford had once met and danced with local girls in the Cairo Club. The club's former owner, Joy Collier, now lived in a mobile home in Wick. She reeled off a list of names.

"Lionel Blair, Anita Roddick, Michael Barrymore, Ringo Starr, we had the famous and infamous," she laughed. "It was one long laugh. Dancing, drinking. And maybe something to eat if you were lucky."

Joy's parents had opened the club for officers just after the Second World War, when the nearby Ford Aerodrome was still operational but later decided to relax the rules.

Joy told me the story: "Daddy said, 'those chief petty officers are spending more than the officers.' So he went to see Commander Aire at Ford and said, 'Would you object if I had the petty officers in as well?' Then when they shut Ford Aerodrome, we had to open it to the locals. They weren't 'officer' material. But they were all good lads. It was a small town, and everybody knew everybody else, and no one was better than anyone else."

Joy ran the Cairo Club until, one day, a millionaire called Michael McGiver walked in.

"He was a lovely man, straight as a die. He said 'How much do you want for it?' I was 74 and worn out. '£400,000, I said, without blinking.' I'd had a wonderful life in that bloody great place but I'd had enough."

Joy sold the club, though the Lemon Tree restaurant it became didn't last. Joy is happy though, living quietly in her park home, with her friend Jeanette in another mobile home not far away, feeding the swans when they wander in to the front garden.

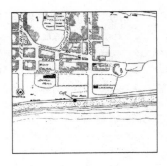

14

Fire dogs and Englishmen

I'd braved the murk of the wettest June on record, to speak to a man about his addiction to fire stations and Littlehampton's in particular. From my window-seat at the East Beach Café on the promenade, I stared at the local entertainment through the glass wall of the cafe. The sea was pure theatre, a living painting.

Thomas Heatherwick, who had gone on to create the Olympic Cauldron for London 2012, had apparently found a piece of wood on the beach on which he'd based the sinuous shape of the café on the prom, where I was now rendezvousing with the fire station fanatic. I imagined Heatherwick exploring the shoreline like Coleridge and Donna, the artist I'd met on West Beach back in January, who sculpted from driftwood. The East Beach Café's design had won awards and column inches in newspapers, as well as being the only place I'd ordered kumquats.

"Thomas said that when we are in the building 'we want prospect but refuge too,'" its owner, Jane Wood, said coming to sit down at my table for a moment to chat. She loved Heatherwick's work and thought he was a "genius".

"For an all-year-round building, it needed to be warm and cosy and protected within," she went on. "Imagine how exposed you'd feel if the other wall was all glass too."

"The sea is different every day," one of the waitresses added. She stood quietly beside my table. Slim and fair, her name was Sylvia and she came from Walbrzych near the landlocked Polish border with the Czech Republic. "You never get bored with the sea." Sylvia said, smiling. "My favourite sea is a winter sea; the sky is a white-greyish colour and the sea is silver and it's calm and quiet and looks just like a picture. It's absolutely beautiful."

Just then, Michael Bissett-Powell arrived and I was soon caught up in his love of fire stations that had begun with a bike ride from Felpham one long-ago summer holiday.

"My father was shell-shocked as well as gassed after his return from the killing fields of First World War Europe. It affected his nerves terribly and my mother couldn't cope with him. In those days, divorce was still out of the question. They were so involved with their own lives and getting from one day to the next that I had to find my own amusement." Seven-year old Michael had been allowed to bring his bicycle on holiday. "It's all flat here, so perfect for cycling. It was great to cut a load of sandwiches in the morning and put them in your Chossy saddlebag and cycle off for the day."

Our fish stew arrived. Between bites, Michael described how he had pedalled the miles, lunchbox in tow, to Littlehampton's old fire station.

"It was a typical hot summer's day and the doors of the station were open. The machine was outside and I was able to look at it and talk to the men."

He had never forgotten that. Years later, he made Christmas cards with hand-painted fire stations on and has researched Littlehampton's fire station with some thoroughness. The earliest record of it Michael had found was the volunteers of July 24th, 1875. There was probably an earlier fire station, he said, somewhere near Beach Road, but he hadn't found it yet on any of the old Ordnance Survey maps he had scoured.

I learned from Michael that in the late 19th and early 20th century, fire stations were the pride of every town, built to a standard and not to a price. Michael explained it was quite advanced for a small town the size of Littlehampton to have any kind of brigade let alone a properly-organised one with regular drills and practices. In the early days, open fire engines were used, so the men sometimes fell off and there were even fatalities.

"But most of the men were sailors," said Michael, "They were used to dealing with heights from climbing the rigging of the sailboats still being used, so they were happy to go up ladders." For parades like the old May Day, the firemen were always there, the engines pulled by horses, likely Michael said, to have been stabled elsewhere, perhaps pulling the local dust cart or the milk float.

"As soon as the 'shout' went up for a fire, the horses would be unclipped from their vehicles. With other fire stations, the horses would sometimes even find their own way from the stable next door and reverse themselves up to the machines, ready to be harnessed. They were as keen as the firemen to get to the blaze and highly intelligent."

Then he said, "Littlehampton's old fire station had its own dog, called Chance." I leaned forward enchanted. "Chance would run ahead, barking to alert people to move aside, clearing a path for the engine. Chance would bark furiously by a door in a burning building, until the firemen broke the door down to discover someone trapped inside."

It was my favourite piece of information from our conversation and one of those nuggets of gold that I stumbled on every so often during my Jigsaw Journey through town.

Michael showed me a picture he had of the two fireboats that had worked the Arun during the war years, the 'Windswept' and the 'Pride of Bognor'. With their own pumps and jets, they played an important role when Littlehampton was used for the rescue mission to Dunkirk, dousing fires in the boat yards that with all the timber and fuel present could have spread like wildfire.

We left the café and, as it was still teeming down, Michael drove us the short distance to Maltravers Road. He pulled in outside the social club opposite the fire station, staring through the rain-dappled windscreen at the ugly, squat building. It was the modern successor to the one Michael had cycled to as a boy sparking his lifelong passion for fire stations.

"The firemen in those days were called by a siren – the old wartime one," he said wistfully. "Now there are pagers for those who are on duty." He harbours dreams of redesigning the building. "It would have very good quarters for the staff. And a smoke alarm. Arundel's fire station didn't and it burnt down." A sobering and bizarre piece of information, I couldn't help but think.

*

Chance the fire dog was long gone, but other dogs now patrolled the environs of the town, many of them coming out for night walks to sniff and snuffle along the promenade with their masters and mistresses. A few days after Michael had told me about Chance's courageous exploits, I was out on the prom. It was dusk. The rain had stopped but a strong easterly was blowing in from the sea.

I had arranged an evening walk along the seafront with another artist, Mark Jolly, as he took his customary evening stroll beside the sea with his dogs.

I'd always loved walking at this hour, at dusk, in the countryside or the city. There was a sense of change and anticipation. The moon was on the rise, and it was what the French call 'l'heure entre le chien et le loup' – the hour between dog and wolf. But this was the Queen's England and there were no wolves howling in the moonlight on the East Greens, just rumours of dragons to the north of the town as well as every shape and breed of dog out scenting the air, yipping, drooling, snarling, being walked, tugging on a lead, trotting jauntily or dragging an owner after it, according to wont.

Mark was waiting with his dogs by the town's 'Longest Bench in the World', that flowed in whirls along the prom in order to get it into the record books by giving it a longer length than it covered on the ground. There was a bit of a rumpus as I arrived.

Mark's dogs were a former breeding pair of short-haired German pointers called Purdy and Bru. At 10 and 11 years old respectively and having reared as many pups between them, Purdy and Bru had earned the right to spend their retirement fruitlessly chasing after seagulls.

"Woof!" A massive hound, punch-drunk on tonight's night-time perambulation, gate-crashed our party and I barked out a rude word before Mark and I had scarcely introduced ourselves. We disentangled ourselves from the intruder and pressed on, the wind snatching my words away and blowing my hair across my face.

"We are facing the south-west, so are getting the easterlies coming in from Scandinavia." Mark tilted his forehead into the teeth of the wind towards the glimmer of light on the horizon, near where the red eye of the light house at Selsey Bill had blinked on.

"How do you know it's coming from Scandinavia? Are you into meteorology?"

"No, it was on the weather forecast last night! Look at the shadows cast by the moonlight and the last gleam on the horizon that's disappearing. It's beautiful, isn't it?"

He was right, it was, the dying rays of the sun slipping down like embers in a guttering fire. I could see shadows on the rollers. Asking him if he liked to paint the water, I was surprised to hear Mark worked with a material that wasn't fluid at all, stone. With his brother Rob, he carved headstones and restored churches and other religious buildings.

"The light's just sort of disappearing and coming across the horizon to pick up the waves," Mark said now. "Things appear rather differently. You've got the sunlight on the flat surface of the wave, but where the rollers are forming you've got an almost black shadow. That's all you can see, the shadow of the waves."

The lighthouse winked again. I'd always loved lighthouses, their look and what they represent, and found Littlehampton sea at night exhilarating. There was something magnificent about a lighthouse against the open sea. Perhaps that was why the town had chosen it for its stone emblem in the past. The surface of the water was white or silver in the moonlight. It was both desolate and uplifting.

"We're on the edge of a heavy raincloud front, so we're getting the light coming through beyond that," Mark said beside me. "I like the silhouettes that it causes when you are looking across the dunes. In the sunrise you get the light coming straight onto the sand, picking the colours up distinctly. But at night, it's just a mound; it's amazing."

Mark grew up here and returned after a five-year stint in Cork in Ireland. "I forgot how much I really appreciate it," he said, taking it in with a deep breath.

We set off again, walking fast. I wasn't sure if it was him or the dogs setting the pace. Living not far from the beach, Mark usually walks around four miles a day, every morning and night, criss-crossing the town and seafront. He loved its wildlife and the migratory birds and the insects of West Beach, with an occasional deer following the line of the river at dusk. It's a link with the old ducal estate that Mark believed would eventually be reclaimed by the sea, with much of the current golf course naturally creating a wildlife reserve, echoing Professor Morton who wanted to see the wetlands brought back.

Mark said Purdy and Bru wanted their customary stroll to Rustington and it would only take about 20 minutes. But I knew I wasn't agile enough to be able to keep up with them, so the four of us, two humans and two dogs, turned away from the wind following the hedge inland along the seafront greens. We were interrupted by the latest canine friend, this one obviously well-known to Mark.

"Hello Maia," he said and she rolled over to have her stomach tickled on the dark grass. I didn't tell him, but Mark reminded me of a long-ago friend, Nick, a fellow art student at university. Nick had talked about the outdoor sculptures he was going to create that would be in the middle of nowhere. People would tramp through fields to get to them. The last I heard of him he'd become a chartered surveyor. Or perhaps like others experiencing 'Shirley Valentine' moments he had moved to the coast and was living somewhere here in Littlehampton.

Because here were two new sculptures, out in the seafront greens. Mark and I paused at the two wooden creatures, an oyster catcher and a crab, carved out of windfall oaks and bolted together. Later, Rosie, from the council, would send me some poems that children from the town had written about the creatures. The children had sat in a circle listening to whispered tales of dark and heroic deeds and come up with events to fit the legend of the Oyster Catcher, which bore a scar on its face. The scar, one child suggested, was a reminder of when the bird tried to steal a pearl from the crab, which lashed out with its pincer.

15

Ticket to Littlehampton

Littlehampton's railway station was my next station stop, as those who work them say. I loved stations almost as much as Michael Bissett-Powell liked fire stations. I wasn't a train spotter, but as a kid I'd hung around them. This was because like the days bobbing in the Merle-Hi beside the jetty, we hadn't ventured far for family holidays. Bournemouth in Dorset was the furthest we had ventured, so as a teenager I used to sit in my local railway station to soak up the atmosphere – not one of the great Victorian junctions, but humble Hove, to watch people coming and going. Since then, I'd travelled on the train all over Europe as far as the Croatian coast, the latter on a night service from Frankfurt in a couchette aboard a great clanking relic from the days of the old Yugoslav Republic.

Littlehampton's station was a terminus, from where you could go anywhere but south. But that wasn't always the case. The original line from the Victorian station built in Lyminster in 1846 had gone west too, to Ford. You can still see an old road bridge over the track at the back of Courtwick Lane Farm in Littlehampton. And you could even travel south in the old days. The route was extended in 1863 from Pulborough to Littlehampton with a triangle of track known as the Arundel Junction to serve the cross-channel ferry passengers. The town got a brand new station in Terminus Road. There was even a shuttle service with fast trains connecting Littlehampton via Ford and Arundel to London, Brighton and Portsmouth. Like so much else, it fell victim to Beeching's infamous railway cuts in the 1960s. But a hundred railway cars are still marshalled in sidings next to the station overnight and two or three thousand people pass through every day.

I was meeting up with Tony, a railway and union man, after the morning rush hour. A solitary figure, already standing outside as I drove slowly past, gave me a cheery wave. I parked hurriedly in the town centre car park nearby, grabbed my notepad and kit bag and set off at a fast stagger. Running was still beyond me but I was no longer trailing wires, though I carried the tens machine as emergency back-up in my bag.

"Would you like a cup of tea?" Tony asked me, very much at home. He paid at the kiosk and carried the two teas over, the steam rising from the styrofoam cups as soon as I lifted the lid to sip it.

"The golden rule," he said as we sat down on the bench by

the ticket office, "is always to place yourself so the sun is in your opposite number's eyes, so you have the advantage." I realised he had manoeuvred me so I was indeed sitting with the sun in my eyes.

I wanted to hear about Tony's early days working on the railways, as I knew he had caught the tail end of the steam age and that the first train he had driven was pulled by a steam locomotive.

"Everything was loaded in at the station. You name it – lions and elephants with Bertram Mills Circus. All the parcels for all the shops used to come here in the yard. Animals like cattle and sheep. Fresh fish came down from places like Hull and Grimsby overnight arriving here in the morning. There was a little fish shop at the end of the station. Some lovely things happened here. At Christmas, both platforms would be absolutely stacked with mail and they'd have Christmas mail trains here full of cards and presents. It's all gone now."

I could see it all in my mind's eye. The whirl of activity on the platform, and heard the whistle blowing. "It must have been great," I replied.

Tony had worked on the timber trains. The timber would come in off the ships into Littlehampton at the crowded docks and was transferred to the builders' merchants on their own trains.

"If you were an engine fireman and you'd done something wrong, the driver would think nothing of giving you a clip round the ear," laughed Tony, taking a sip of tea. "But we never dropped each other in it. We covered up for each other. We were like a family. It was a hard life, but a brilliant life.

We had railway clubs and first-aid competitions. Now it's just a corporate machine."

Together with three other firemen or stokers, Tony would unload four 16-tonne trucks of coal by hand, ready for the night coalman to coal up the engines.

"We never thought anything of it," he said, though he later worked for a haulage firm and joined a trades union. But Tony said Littlehampton was never a red hotbed of trade unionism, down here on the south coast. "It's all small businesses here," he said by way of explanation.

Paul from Paul's Station Snacks came over to say hello. He leased the kiosk six days a week and was here every day except Sundays at 5.30am sharp, making fresh sandwiches.

"It's nice and buzzy," Paul said chattily. "People are normally happy except when there's a problem with the trains." He used to work late shifts as an insurance agent but much preferred this. "It has a much better atmosphere than driving around in my car."

Paul left us to serve a customer and Tony and I set off to have a look around the station, which had won Southern's 'best small medium station category,' something that had clearly made the supervisor's day.

The very last London, Brighton & South Coast locomotive or steam train shed was at Littlehampton. I followed Tony into the old shed where a previous canteen had also once been, and the parcel and booking office. At that time it had just been freshly painted.

"The rails and the pits are still under here," said Tony mysteriously.

Once, soon after he'd first started working on the railways, Tony's driver went home to dinner, leaving him to pull the locomotive out of the sidings alone. But the engine 'caught its water', which happened if the boilers were dirty and sucked the water up into the cylinders and the engine started moving of its own accord.

"When that happened, the thing would go off like a greyhound!" grinned Tony. "That time, the guard hadn't pulled the points back. The train hit the buffers and a piece of rail was knocked off and went clean through a car belonging to one of the coalmen. It slid along the back seat and out the other side. No one was in it but it was six weeks before the driver got any coal at home. Not until the coalman got his insurance pay-out for a new car."

Tony had also been the guard aboard the ill-fated service that left Littlehampton at 12:17 on May 4th, 1989. Six people died in what became known as the Purley train crash. Tony was relatively lucky. Apart from damaging his hearing in the crash, he was unscathed. He told me the driver of the train, Bob Morgan, had been convicted for manslaughter that was overturned on appeal 18 years later.

Tony sighed: "Bob later drowned in a sailing accident. He wasn't a very lucky lad. Poor old Bob."

We left the station heading along the main road which Tony said was laid when the road bridge to Bognor was built, more than 20 years back. The gas station lay hulking against the horizon. It is not a gasometer, but has a giant bag effectively in it that stores gas for the town.

Tony had been on it. "It used to have a watchman there. When it was being built, I actually walked on the top of it. You can see Chichester cathedral from there."

We passed the old signal boxes that used to have oil lamps at the top, changed every week by a travelling lamp man whose business was also to light the lamps in Arundel, as well as the nearby villages of Burpham, Angmering and Ford. Tony pointed out the houses that lined the back of the tracks away from the road.

"They were railwaymen's cottages when the railways were first built up, until a few years ago. They've all been gradually sold off. The end ones were foreman's houses. There are more in the back streets. The railwaymen would climb over the wall into the Steam Packet for their dinner and a couple of pints."

Suddenly, a telepathic warning flashed up in my head and I forgot all about the railwaymen shinning over the wall for a pint in the pub. "We have to go back to my car," I urged, "as quick as we can." In my haste not to keep Tony waiting when I'd seen him already standing outside the station, I'd forgotten to reset my car-parking clock on the dashboard. We hurried back, just seconds too late. A warden had just entered the number plate into his little hand-held machine for a £25 penalty notice. Even with sixth sense, you can't win 'em all.

*

There are ghostly imprints of older versions of Littlehampton superimposed on newer ones all over town. Once, the Electric Picture Palace or the Regent, as it was in a later incarnation, had thrived opposite the station here. It was the town's last original picture house and is now a block of flats. Another one called the Palladium used to operate in Church Street and is now also a block of flats called Amenic Court. Cinema backwards is a nice twist for lovers of anagrams. The Odeon in the High Street is a bookshop.

You can still enjoy a film at the independent Windmill theatre on the seafront. The Windmill launched its cinematic career to a sharp intake of breath with *Working Girl*, a film I used to watch whenever I was fed up or in need of a reminder that David can sometimes beat Goliath. It turned out to be a prediction for the Windmill's own survival, thanks to a determined fight by its supporters to keep it. In the 1980s, dignitaries were scandalized by Melanie Griffith fleeing the backseat of a limo where a lecherous boss is playing blue movies on his in-car video.

I crossed Terminus Road and went into the Steam Packet pub, as I'd promised myself I'd do back in February. I ordered a filter coffee. The new owner, Mark Pester, a builder and publican who was restoring the pub, showed me black and white framed photos taken more than a century ago. In one, a postman stood in the sun, a bicycle leaning against the pub wall (*see photos*). From the man's shadow, Mark had worked out that the date and time was 4pm in high summer. Another photograph showed a view of the Steam Packet from Rope Walk. In the foreground was the river and the infamous chain ferry, a coalman aboard with his horse and loaded cart, heading for the western bank and the Portsmouth Road. Perhaps he had just had a swift pint at the Packet. Just visible over his shoulder was a sign with the tempting words 'Fine Old and Mild Ales.' Mark told me the free house used to be a thatched barn before it was bought by a trio of brewers from Brighton in 1870. Some of the barn's original flint walls still remain inside.

16

Up and down the High Street

Back in January when I had first tried walking up the High Street, it was an enormous feat to get my feet up the relatively gentle slope, past Bunce's hardware store, formerly Ockendon's, the oldest family business in town. Every Tuesday, I helped out in Barnardo's charity shop at the bottom of the slope, as a way of avoiding dropping entirely out of the world. There had been a high stool to sit on at the till and the manageress, who had a cartilage issue, and I swapped gossip on the natural remedies for knees with names like devil balm and dragon blood that could have as easily been heavy metal bands, like other women shared make-up tips.

I had been using an old exercise bike stuck on one gear that had been rigged up for the purpose in my mother's garage. Doing just one minute had initially been a struggle. I had tried to push myself, overdone it, regretted it, then lost all confidence and avoided the thing ever since. But under hospital physiotherapist Mark's watchful eye, I'd been working out on equipment.

In Arcade Road, just off the bottom of the High Street, was a small gym frequented by tattooed bodybuilders. I had often glimpsed them congregating outside the entrance to the gym. I decided I was going to progress from Bognor Hospital's small gym and go in the one on Arcade Road. It seemed to me that if I could overcome my natural reserve to go in the gym, I would be overcoming other inner doubts, such as would I ever really run again. I wasn't an athlete but I had done some fun runs in my time and missed being able to go jogging and cycling. It turned out to be a wise choice. In a big, plush gym, awash with lycra, I would not have had the support and attention that Neil, a former London bailiff-turned-gym owner, artist and bodybuilding contestant, gave me.

On my first visit, I tentatively pulled the bar down with a 5lb weight. Neil gave me a light workout to follow.

"Just something to get the blood flowing through your back." Neil knew his stuff. Under his tutelage, I put on boxing gloves and hit a pad that he held, then a punch bag, connecting my fists with it in a satisfying manner, imagining the solar plexus of the consultant who'd given me the epidural in Paris. The gym was to become a regular stop on my itinerary.

*

I'd finished another session at the gym, where I had tried and managed a heavy-footed jogging for a few minutes on Neil's single treadmill. It was market day and now I was standing on a corner of one of the cut-throughs off the High Street, reading about the smugglers who were once as much a part of Littlehampton as its river. A curlicued write-up on the outside wall of the shop in which the South Coast Pasty Company now operate, boasted of smugglers resting there after supplying the Crown Inn next door with contraband. It told of a large bell attached to the side of the building that had been rung to warn when the coast literally was clear and the customs officers had gone. Apparently, there had been secret tunnels and passageways running between the shore and the Crown in those days in which gin, rum, tobacco and thousands of gallons of French brandy were smuggled in at a fraction of its trade price.

I went into the shop to get a pasty. I had lost track as to whether it was late breakfast or early lunch. "I'll have that one." I pointed at a salmon pasty and watched the girl on the till snare it expertly with tongs and lower it into a bag. In the meantime, she told me about the shop's resident ghost – yet another one – that might have been a smuggler and was certainly a seafarer. The story went that one Black Joan, brother to Finn and the more violent of the two, was said to have murdered a deckhand for cheating at poker.

"The deckhand is still waiting for his return ship that will never come," said the server, finishing her tale.

I took the warm package and sat on a bench outside the shop to eat it, keeping an eye on the nearby clock tower as I munched my pasty, as that was where I had arranged to meet not one but two of Littlehampton's old market gaffers.

Deano and Maggie had been 'gaffers' in charge of the old indoor market in Surrey Street and had agreed to join me for a wander through the new market that took over Littlehampton High Street on Fridays. Together, the three of us weaved our way among the stalls, Deano and Maggie greeting friends every so often. Deano walked with a stick after losing an arm more than 30 years ago. We wandered past a butcher, what I would come to know later as 'the egg man', florist and green grocer, as well as stalls selling dog baskets, mittens, MP3 players and cheap socks and knickers. A Romany woman held out bunches of lavender to us for luck, as they have done for generations. Mobility scooters interwove the pedestrians. Deano liked the market and thought it would bring new life to the town.

"It needs a bit more space to spread out," objected Maggie.

Their children had grown up in the markets, with other stallholders minding them, all one big family and they knew their business well. We did a circuit noticing the changing times had closed some shops and opened others, with new cafés amongst them with their tables and chairs outside. Deano showed me an outside wall painted black where he told me a mural of local shoppers used to be.

We retired to the Weatherspoons pub on Surrey Street. The pub had more framed photographs of old Littlehampton on its walls.

"The secret to a successful market," said Deano, "is in the variety of the stallholders, getting those unusual things that people can't get anywhere else." Like the outsize clothing stall at the market he'd run. "It did everything for the larger lady, from cardis to summer dresses. It was fashion clothing," said Deano, "and very popular. Then there was 'the egg man' and the women who sold everything you ever needed or wanted for cleaning."

Over coffee, I was reminded not for the first time that in a town this size, it can be a very small world and everybody knew each other. In this case, Maggie, Deano's wife, was the stepdaughter of Peter Davis', aka the Old Bugger, who ran the little chandlery over on Rope Walk. That would have been why the Old Bugger had suggested it.

*

I said goodbye to Maggie and Deano, then wandered back down the High Street through the Arcade Road. On the other side was a bijou little square, called Spark's Court, with a handful of shops on it. One of them was 'Way Out There and Back'. The name was from JRR Tolkien's The Hobbit and the shop sold birthstones, crystals, fairy gates and joss sticks as well as organic herbs and vegetables, some of the seedlings propagating on the sunny window sill. If you didn't know the square was there, you might miss it. I'd first gone in there for a meditation CD to learn more patience, and come out with a set of wind chimes and a large floret of purple broccoli. More recently, Staci and Dave who own it had taken to running a weekend market in the tiny square where people could sell craft goods while raising money for a children's charity. Jah, the ex-cabbie, a jobbing double-bass player called Harry and me would be providing the live music at one of them.

Dave, who had been born in Bulawayo, Rhodesia's second city, before the country became Zimbabwe, was tending his seedlings of sage, parsley and purple basil when I went in.

"Hello there!" Staci greeted me in her usual friendly fashion. She was American, and her grandmother had run a speakeasy; Staci had a big personality and grew sunflowers, juicy tomatoes and strawberries, very different to Dave's understated and quieter herbs. She had run a restaurant in London some years back, but took up the family trade after her mother bought and converted the little shop, a former hairdresser's salon.

"I stayed away from palmistry and tarot and I fought it all the way," Staci said with a lift of her chin. "But the restaurant put me in hospital too many times with peptic ulcers." She told me she had fallen in love with the shop and the courtyard as soon as she saw them, in the centre of town, but still tucked away.

Staci had since embraced her fate and written several books on tarot with Dave, as no doubt the cards could have told her, had she not avoided them. A pair of budgies were tweeting happily behind the counter. Before them, Staci kept a pet mynah bird in the shop. But the naughty bird acquired some colourful language.

"That bird had a habit of talking dirty. He made inappropriate comments to customers. He was aggressive to brunettes and possessive whenever I served male customers." The mynah bird had also talked roguishly in the presence of

Daisy, who now lay dozing in the shop. But Daisy, a cross between an Alsatian and a Rhodesian Ridgeback, didn't mind. The Ridgebacks had been originally bred as fighting dogs, but Daisy was the runt of her litter and wouldn't hurt a fly. Staci and I arranged the date for my little trio to play at her market. She was organising eight of them. I was promised sandwiches and tea on tap in return for our playing two sets of jazz standards.

*

Rather like a latter day version of Mr Benn, the children's character, I slipped out of 'Way Out There And Back' and entered another door with an equally enticing name above it, the 'Silk Road Restaurant' writ large on its frontage. But here it was mezes on the menu and Turkish coffee rather than dandelion tea and purple broccoli. The restaurant sometimes had belly dancers. It had thick, heavy curtains hanging to the tiled floors, and a trompe l'oeil of a souk on the wall. There were little corners to hide away in. It felt like an oasis in the desert brought by the genie's lamp to barely a camel's ride from Littlehampton's post office in the arcade across the road. Years ago, the Silk Road's owner Teresa Esfahani ran another Turkish restaurant, for a well-known Turk in north London.

"I was devoted to him," Teresa said. She had just come back with fresh garlic, parsley, mint, mushrooms and cream from her daily shop and was about to type up the evening's menu. "He was very short, very fat. A playboy with a stubby finger in every pie, very well known in the Turkish community. But for all his faults, he oozed character and charm and the staff loved him. He made people feel the party hadn't begun till you walked in the room."

Teresa did not have a drop of Turkish blood but had once been married to an Iranian, learning about perfume and colour in Persian cuisine from her in-laws. I'd had a lot of Iranian friends in Paris who had fled the 1979 Revolution, and one had told me that when you cook rice in the Persian tradition you have to make it dance. But Iranian chefs were far more difficult to come by, so the Silk Road Restaurant offered Turkish and Mediterranean dishes.

"Iranian women have a way of understanding how to get the flavour out of simply frying an onion," smiled Teresa. "Where to begin in a dish and how to draw out the oils, flavours and tastes of each ingredient. What to add to it without covering up what you've already done but to build on those flavours, like smoking and crushing an aubergine to get the taste out of it. They grow up around kitchens like we used to. Dad goes out and picks the aubergine and parsley from the shop. Mum is at home chopping up the onions. Everything is fresh. We used to be like that."

The kitchen was already at work and a pleasing aroma of warming spices was drifting in, just like the first night I'd come here.

*

The first time I'd gone out on my own in the evening after my injury, I had felt nervous. I knew almost no one in Littlehampton, so had gee'd myself up to go to a meeting of the Silk Road Writers at the restaurant on Arcade

Road I had seen advertised. The medics had warned me not to stay sitting for too long in one position, to stop my leg going back into a spasm or my back seizing up. I had bobbed up and down all night like a yoyo. Even worse, I had brought along my trusty cushion, the dreaded doughnut that embarrassed everyone but me. I had built up quite a collection of therapeutic cushions for my various coccyx injuries over the years. But none were in the league of the round doughnut another French hospital had given me after I'd broken my coccyx falling off the runaway horse in Provence. The French gave the doughnuts to patients who were pregnant, had piles or both – and me. While still on the mend, I had gone to a restaurant at a casino in Brighton and the hostess had inquired in all sincerity: "Would you like me to take your hat, madam?"

Now here I was again at the Silk Road Writers' meeting. Many faces had changed. Writers who drift in and out of the group had come along as well as some regulars. Paul, the pub pianist who had run the group last time I'd been, wasn't there. The women all had ethereal and folky names like Rilla and Lilias. Tonight, the men were all called David – almost to a man!

Lilias's great grandfather was Henry Rider Haggard, who had written the novel *She* on which the 1965 film was based and from it the phrase "she who must be obeyed" was apparently coined.

Lilias was a free spirit, who had spent months living in a plastic polytunnel in Wales, after falling in love with a ranger, and then in a tent in London as a protestor against social injustice. Since I had seen her, she had let all the grey in her long hair grow through and there were gaps in her smile revealing the odd missing molar.

"Like the Crosby, Stills, Nash and Young song, I'm flying my freak flag and proud of it," she beamed, speaking in her lovely, soft, old-fashioned West Sussex burr and showing off the gaps.

That night we each read the lyrics from a Beatles' song.

"Take away the tune and there's still a rhythm and the words all fit together. They might be repetitious, but they are poems too," said one David.

Another David read the words aloud from *Yesterday*. It sounded even bleaker as a poem.

A third David said: "I'm not a writer, but a painter. What I enjoy is hearing an extension to my visual experience by hearing language being used live. People talking about words and expressions and ideas. That extends my own interpretation of things." He showed me some of his paintings, that were surprisingly fiery, in deep reds and magentas.

The first David told me he had contributed to the group's book of poems about the town. "I went around and took some photographs of iconic places and put some words to them. The clock outside Sainsbury's. The jeweller's pawn shop. The war memorial." Was it a poetic place or somewhere that needed poetry, I wondered. Perhaps a bit of both.

17

Read all about it!

"I guess these things have to be done," Roger Green shouted cheerfully above the roar of the traffic grinding its way up the contraflow. "The Victorian cast iron gas mains need replacing and I'd rather that than have the road blown up."

I'd first encountered Roger, editor of the *Littlehampton Gazette*, the town's long-established weekly newspaper, when I'd gone up to his first-floor office unknowingly trailing wires like a bridal train behind me, as one of the tens machine's suckers had become detached. I had found Roger the gentleman editor personified, a character straight out of a Graham Greene novel, dapper and never out of a suit and tie, even in 40 degrees. He had an unhurried way of speaking, which I had initially found unnerving after the point-scoring banter from all the opinionated mavericks clamouring for attention in the big newsrooms I'd worked in from London to Paris.

Now Roger had agreed to accompany me along the Beach Road leg of my journey through town, where the *Gazette's* offices had been for decades, for the first 50 years on one side of the road, then the other.

"It's probably the longest-running business in town," Roger said mildly after we had set off at an amiable dawdle. He told about all the places he had worked, starting out as a cub reporter on The Sentinel, an evening paper in Staffordshire, then further north covering the Toxteth riots as well as Everton and Liverpool football matches.

"Fancy being paid to watch the league and European football," Roger chortled, as we strolled down Beach Road together. It was a Friday, the day after the paper came out, and there were no deadlines to worry about.

Roger had also worked as a political correspondent in Bath and at a Christian news magazine for young readers called Buzz. "That taught me how to write five-page features."

"What's the secret?" I asked, feeling I might need it.

"Observation, asking questions, digging a bit deeper, really get under the skin of the story and the people," Roger replied in a beat.

His last job before the *Littlehampton Gazette* was in the Midlands, where his first story was covering the end of the miners' strike in 1984 as the workers marched proudly back to the pits behind their colliery band.

"One of those occasions that sends a tingle up your spine."

"A moment in history?"

"Yes, it was."

More than a decade after the day on which the men marched back to the mines, Roger was interviewed for the post of editor on the *Littlehampton Gazette*. His 'interrogators' had leaned forward and asked him a question, "If you nipped out for a sandwich or to get a tenner from the cashpoint, how long would you be?"

Roger replied he'd be at least half-an-hour because he would keep stopping to talk to people.

"If you know your patch and the people on the patch know you, they will stop you and say, 'Roger, I want to have a word with you. What about the hospital? Have you heard this shop is closing down? Or, 'my mother can't get the treatment she needs at her GP surgery'. And that's how it should be." His first act as the new editor was to write an open letter asking for Government funds to regenerate the town, which they got. "Since then, the town has begun to recover," Roger thought. Iceland, Lidl, WH Smith, Greggs the Bakers and Waitrose had opened alongside long-established family businesses and independent shops like Spokes Cycles, Dean Carpets and Arun Furnishers on Beach Road. Sure, some businesses didn't last. But in a town like Littlehampton, where rents are not too high, it is a good place to try something different, take a risk, do that thing you have always wanted to do, like Neil's sloop, like Alan Thomas' bed and breakfast.

"If it works it works, and if it doesn't, maybe you haven't lost too much," said Roger.

We passed a Polish supermarket. "There's quite a large European community here," Roger was saying. "There's a hairdresser and a supermarket run by people from the former East European bloc. It seems to be doing very well," he gestured at the supermarket. Before that, Portuguese and Moroccan communities had grown up, coming for work on farms and in the glass houses. People from Poland, Lithuania, Latvia and Russia were the most recent to come to Littlehampton.

"They need somewhere they can get what they like to eat and enjoy," Roger said.

I remembered missing tea that wasn't in a Lipton's sachet in Paris, along with McVitie's Digestives and a decent curry. Then I had found a splendid store called Le Bon Marché on the Left Bank, that specialised in foods from around the world and proudly displayed marmite and Heinz Baked Beans in its British section. Now I missed olive oil soap from Marseilles, celeriac remoulade, the wonderful patisserie shops with their exquisite savoury delicacies and cakes and still thought of chicory as endives. A little street sweeper van tore past us on the corner by the photographer's showroom of brides and babies as if it were into the final lap of the Grand Prix. Another dustcart followed, a larger one, this one at a respectable pace.

At the end of Beach Road near where it meets Arcade Road, is a Chinese restaurant called Chopsticks. Peter, its friendly chef, worked out at Neil's gym. When he wasn't lifting weights alongside me he was explaining how to cook Chinese food, telling me such things as how to use water in a wok rather than oil, in between rounds with his weights. Then after our work-out he would send over healthy, steam-cooked rice and vegetable meals, topped with an egg for protein, for our lunch at the gym.

"Oh, hello," said Roger as Andrew Sleeman, the owner of Spokes bicycles, came out of his shop. Andrew was a volunteer on the lifeboat and a founding member of a partnership for local traders in the town. The two fell into lively conversation. Roger knew everyone and his working principle of being away for half an hour from the office still held good.

I was sad when, some while later, I heard that Roger was retiring. It was the end of an era and a loss to the town and the *Gazette*. The paper is still going strong but has not renewed its lease on its office in the town after first opening in Littlehampton in 1893.

The *Gazette's* former neighbours at 36, Beach Road had once churned out thousands of prints of a very different nature to the weekly news. It was the erstwhile hub of Britain's saucy seaside postcard industry. Artist Donald McGill's cards had once been on sale in seaside shops along the south coast while hundreds had been banned by council censors in the north of England, stamped with the word 'disapproved'. A shopkeeper here in Arundel Road had tipped me the wink that the company which owned the copyright for the cards, D Constance Ltd, had moved from Beach Road to a "shed with a corrugated roof" at 2, High Street, before going bust – all puns intended. While the owner of a postcard museum told me administrators had approached the owner of a junk shop in Littlehampton to unload all the cards, with their henpecked husbands, buxom wives and rosy-cheeked vicars. The story goes that the junk-shop owner made thousands: more than double the debts of the bankrupt company. Littlehampton Museum bought some of the postcards and one or two of the old printing press plates.

18

The Mayor of Mewsbrook Park

The sunlight filtering through the high cloud looked like it was off the film set of a biblical drama, as I made my way along the stretch of seafront where I'd practised walking earlier in the year. Today, the sea shimmered and looked very green. A fine rain was falling, putting me in mind of one of my favourite poems by Siegfried Sassoon: 'Warm rain on drooping roses, pattering showers that soak the woods.' I clamped a tea cosy hat on, catching sight of Alan waiting for me at the park gates. Alan had twice been the town's mayor and Mewsbrook Park was a favourite place for him to be alone with his thoughts. He had been born in Streatham in south London, and loved to take refuge in this green oasis on the edge of town, that had been a water meadow in the 16th century. At that moment, it seemed to have found its own again as a rain garden. Well, I had done a night walk, I thought, as Alan and I set off together to walk around the perimeter of the park. This was a rain walk in a rain garden.

"That's gunnera, a member of the rhubarb family, but it's decorative, not edible," said Alan, pointing. He knew a great deal about plants and as soon as he uttered the words herbaceous perennials I knew I was out of my depth, even though that very morning I had picked and eaten a cherry tomato from my mother's garden with a packet of crisps grown in someone else's. Alan had run a garden business and quickly identified aquiligeia with its golden florets making it look like mini tall-stemmed cauliflowers, buddleia and cow-parsley, a rather graceful weed poking its way through the conventional shrubbery. We wandered along the flower borders. Because of the rain, we had the park to ourselves. The flowers had a dishevelled appeal, their rain-dimpled petals and blooms fluttering and stirring in the breeze. Both plants and humans had been fooled into thinking mid-July was summer. But Alan told me he thinks plants like grass are very clever.

"Many of them just shut themselves down when they need to, like when there's drought. They just shut their stems down and go to sleep."

Mewsbrook doubtless owed its continued existence to being unsuitable for building on, or it would no doubt have disappeared long ago. Years ago, Alan said, there were more streams in Littlehampton. A man-made lake was created in the park in 1939, fed by an underground rife at its northern end emerging as a brook, being originally part of the Arun's estuary. At the seaside end, it has an overflow pipe and runs down when it reaches sea-level on, appropriately, Sea Road, by a specially-constructed groyne topped at the end by a marker post called a 'dolphin'. The lake is not freshwater but brackish, with seawater in all probability seeping in through the deeper layers of sand on the beach and through the high tides mixing with the freshwater from the brook.

Several breeds of birds spend the summer in the park, assembling their nests in the banks of the lake, like the house martins we saw. There were also cormorants, swifts and swallows. I have always had a soft spot for swifts, ever since I had learned more about their habits from doing a report on them for the TV programme *Countryfile* some years ago. They are more like bats than birds, with their curved claws designed for clinging on to rock faces and the sides of buildings. We had filmed a swift family that had made its home in a church steeple, flying in and out through the louvre-shutters of the pointed arch window.

Alan's favourites in the park were the swallows. "On a warm summer's evening like this, it's nice to watch them." He scanned the horizon. "They swoop down, skimming the lake here, drinking the water. If we get a mild spring they might arrive as early as late April and not leave until September." During the springtime Alan has watched them flying west every day along the coast until the time comes for them to head for Dungeness, to cross the Channel at the shortest stretch en route to migrating south.

Next we found a pair of coots building a nest, seeming to tug reeds from its base to reposition at its top. The nest was beautifully made, a piece of craftsmanship, like a blackbird nest I had once found in a jasmine bush in the garden with its single egg and what seemed to be a piece of chiffon entwined with the twigs. Now the lake was busy with the feisty coots chasing a swan and mallards from the still-empty nest. Further round the lake, we came across a family of recently hatched ducklings.

Little shelters were dotted about the park, original art deco structures like on the prom, with round 'windows' like serving hatches that made Alan think of ice cream.

We settled down for a bit in one of them and watched the jewelled dragonflies darting about their mysterious business.

"I never thought I'd be the mayor of any town," he said. "It's amazing. Sometimes you speak up for everyone in the town, all 30,000."

Alan showed me the rest of the route he used to walk with his mum past the Ruby Garden named in honour of the Queen Mother's ruby wedding anniversary and forty years of marriage to George VI: past the garden then along the miniature railway track when the train wasn't running. Walking along the railway line on a frosty morning was his favourite time, as it reminded him of the London parks he loved before he came here, to Mewsbrook. This wasn't just any old municipal park to him. This was Mewsbrook Park!

"Mewsbrook has that little something the other parks haven't got," Alan said affectionately. "You can never get fed up with coming here. There's always something different to see, like the variety of plants in the flowerbeds."

We agreed to meet again and walk along the railway tracks later in the year, on a frosty morning as was his wont, with a cup of hot chocolate at the end as a reward.

Not far away from Mewsbrook Park is Parkside Avenue, the next piece in the jigsaw picture I was assembling. I was walking in the town, regularly visiting the little gym on Arcade Road under Neil's tutelage. Summer was having one last riotous fling before softening into autumn, with the 'golden rod' Alan had pointed out blazing in gardens and on railway embankments. The tang of barbecuing sausages and the pealing of church bells carried faintly, now more distinctly, on the breeze. A familiar friend, a male blackbird with its bright yellow beak, perched on our garden wall singing a long, sweet song. I'd picked up the next stage of my walk from the point where I had waved goodbye to Alan at the top end of the park. Or rather, David was walking and I was trotting in his shadow, trying to keep up with his brisk pace. Commander John Kerans had once lived at 19, Parkside Avenue. David Slade, whom I'd met at the Silk Road Writers' meeting remembered the story of Commander Kerans' exploits, because although he had only been five years old, his dad was in the Navy and his family had paid attention to every scrap of news about the British fleet.

To get to the Kerans' old rental abode, David led me on a circuit up Tideway past newer residential streets named for water. We passed Thames Close, Finisterre Way, Lundy Close, Neptune Way and my favourite, White Horses Way. They reminded me of the year I'd worked as an announcer on BBC Radio 4, reading the shipping bulletin. I remembered being petrified I was going to overrun and 'crash' the 'pips' that preceded the news on the hour – which I had done the third time I'd read it – as it all has to be perfectly to time.

It was in a radio broadcast that David and his family heard how Commander John Kerans had saved the ship HMS *Amethyst* in the Yangtze Incident during the 1949 Chinese Revolution. The *Amethyst* had been on a mission on the Yangtze River to evacuate European nationals but then got caught in the fighting between nationalist and communist forces. It was fired on and sustained terrible casualties with loss of life and many wounded. Among the casualties was the ship's brave surgeon who was killed while operating on the wounded.

Under Kerans' command, in a story that made headlines around the world, the ship made a spectacular dash for freedom and the open sea, at one point pumping out thick black smoke to confuse the enemy gunners on the riverbanks. Kerans succeeded and rejoined the rest of the British fleet. His message sent out afterwards ended with 'God save the King.' Among the crew which survived the exploits was Able Seaman Simon, the ship's cat.

We reached the house in Parkside Avenue, not far from the corner of St Flora's Road, to which Kerans had eventually returned home from China and the sea, in the company of a welcome party.

"The family car, an open-topped tourer, had been rigged up with drag-lines by the local sea cadets," David said now. "Having towed the car with his wife in it to the station, they then proceeded to walk it to a reception for the young naval hero at the civic offices."

David gives talks about the *Amethyst* but agrees not many know the name of John Kerans. He puts it down to the British psyche. "We laud people for a limited period of time," he said, "and then the generation moves on. But, in my opinion, you ignore history at your peril."

*

A few days later I had a visit from an old friend. Liz had visited loyally since I had first been injured, driving down from her flat in west London to the hospital. She had later grown to love Littlehampton's clean, wide-open seafront and had a special fondness for Pier Road and the fish and chip shops at which she would invariably stop.

Now, she and I lay in our deck chairs on the prom, the chairs as low and flat as they would go, so that our upturned faces faced the heavens. I had already set down a flask and a packet of biscuits. To all intents and purposes, our deckchair routine, conducted in mid August, was perfectly normal. Except that it was nearly midnight. Liz always scorned coats unless it was a blizzard, but I had a fleece wrapped round me like a kaftan and there was good, hot tea in our flask. If any other late-night loiterer not interested in astronomy wondered what on earth we were about, they were too polite to ask. We were hoping to see a meteor shower over the sea. They were visible on clear nights at this point in the year. But though we sat sipping our increasingly tepid tea in the pitch black for more than an hour, we didn't see a thing. In another August, in another deckchair, alone in a garden, I was lucky enough to see a dozen shooting stars streaking across the sky in the midnight hour. It was breath-taking and magical. But that was a moment in the future.

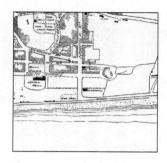

19

Beach Town

I was looking forward to exploring Beach Town, running from where Surrey House – a fine, old house with a scandalous past – used to be at the end of South Terrace, up to where Norfolk Road joins the road to Rustington.

"Where are we actually?" I asked my companion, Dr Ian Friel.

"We're, oh dear, we're ..." Dr Friel hesitated, revealing a charmingly scatty academic side. The historian and a former curator of the town museum continued, "ten years ago, it would have all been at my fingertips, but –"

I consulted my trusty little AA map. "It's Western Road and St Augustine Road."

Beach Town had been the first purpose-built holiday area in the town, developed from the time of the Beach Coffee House of Little Hampton, which had opened in the last quarter of the 18th century, catering for fashionable visitors after the Royals of the day set the trend for horse-drawn sea-bathing in Sussex. One writer who travelled to Beach Town then was Peregrine Phillips, a man who wrote about his experiences in a journal with a very long title!

Diary Kept in an Excursion to Little Hampton, near Arundel and in Sussex in 1778: and Brighthelmston, in Sussex, in 1778; And Also to the Latter Place in 1779.

The latter place, Brighthelmston was the original name for Brighton.

Ian said: "When Peregrine Phillips came here there would have been just the Beach Coffee House and a few huts then nothing. The village of Hampton would have been clustered round the High Street and Surrey Street."

Beach Town's early development was almost certainly promoted by the then Duke of Norfolk. You can see a remnant of planning, particularly at Norfolk Road. "If you stand at the crossroads, you'll see a partial 'grid' pattern," said Ian. He was convinced the Dukes of Norfolk later prevented development in the 19th century, which he said would probably have put a few backs up at the time.

"But it has given Littlehampton a sea frontage that's distinctive, that a lot of other places on the Sussex coast don't have. Worthing and Brighton have wall-to-wall buildings with just a few gaps."

We moved on to explore the terraced houses in Western Road that were purpose-built in the 1850s. Narrow but deep, as boarding houses, they were intended to contain as many rooms as possible to maximise the number of boarders they could take in.

Ian loved the long, slanting sunlit streets in this part of town. There was a Bohemian air about the place, with peeling paint on the walls of some buildings. Beach Town was the 'arty' end of town, what passed in Littlehampton for its equivalent of Paris's Left Bank, the drowsy notes of a saxophone drifting down from an open first floor window.

We crossed the road to Norfolk Road, going back in time to the earliest part of Beach Town. This was where servants from the large houses of South Terrace probably lived, like Surrey Cottage, that had survived the grand house of the same name. The Earl of Berkley had built Surrey House for a milkmaid who was his mistress to live in before they were married. The house was gone but an early 19th century notebook discreetly recorded it as 'the place where the Countess of Berkley lived before her title was recognised.'

Still on Norfolk Place we passed flint cottages in-filled with what Ian called 'galleting'.

"It's where you put little sharp chips of flint in between the larger flint stones. It's decorative, but also helps protects the mortar."

Sometimes you see the downmarket version of galleting with the shards of old bottles among the pebbles. Ian thought it must have been a time-consuming process.

We resumed our stroll in the late summer sunshine, admiring the Georgian buildings in South Terrace. The elegant boulevard had been one of the first to be numbered and receive post! One had an original portico. Look closer and you'll see the pattern of alternating colour bricks: the yellow bricks imported, said Ian, unlike the red 'stretchers' and the burnt 'headers' at the end of the row where the brickmaker oxidised his materials to create decorative patterns.

At the back of South Terrace was an alley near a little self-service laundrette Ian said had been there for years. The backs of the houses had their best brick faces seawards, with the cheaper flint at the sides and rear end. We passed a hairdressing salon, Malcolm's Hair Space, that looked like a time-capsule from the 1970s, its shiny hoods and hairdryers resplendent and waiting for the week's perms. On the corner further along, coloured glass and tile had been used to make glittery mosaics of a sea horse and an octopus in a little garden.

We'd worked our way along Selbourne Road passing a small copse of trees on a triangle of land called Lobbs Wood, which Ian explained was named after a play by J M Barrie. Barrie used to holiday in Rustington with a family whom he was supposed to have based his characters from Peter Pan on. Barrie knew the town well. On a return visit in 1917 during the First World War, he was depressed to see all the new villas and expressed the wish that the Germans come and shell them all.

"Littlehampton is an interesting and unusual place in many ways," Ian added thoughtfully before we parted. His quirkiness and deep knowledge about Beach Town had uncovered glimpses of the past for me where I'd not expected to find them, so typical of Littlehampton as a whole.

20

From Littlehampton with Love

Just up the road from Beach Town lived Bill Thomas. I had once been told 'that London has as many Russian spies as it had during the Cold War. Littlehampton still had at least one – Bill – now retired.

Bill lived in East Street. Bill's old intelligence unit, the 30 Assault Unit, had been stationed here during the war. Its presence had seeped into the fabric of the town. The pub in Selbourne Road was called 'The Marine' and for many years, the sign of a marine in uniform jacket and white trousers hung there, until the pub closed. On a blustery day that whipped my hair across my face and the waves into boisterous white horses that crashed into spray out on East Beach, I walked along South Terrace to the unit's former headquarters on the corner of St Augustine Road. It had been split into flats, as evidenced by a row of bells at the front door.

I called on Bill one chilly afternoon. Mayor Alan's swallows must be on their way south.

"Every morning we had a full parade," Bill told me. Grey light filtered into the room as I listened to Bill telling me how a block of flats now stood in the tennis court that had been the 30 AU's parade ground. "After parade," said Bill, "one or two of us would have skipped off during the night. Gone to do a job. Down to Tangmere to catch a plane or down the river for a boat. Skip across the water, do what they had to do, then come back."

The unit was under the command of Ian Fleming, the creator of James Bond and Chitty Chitty Bang Bang. One of the 30 AU's officers was the dashing Lieutenant Commander Patrick Dalzel-Job. Bill thought he was the main inspiration for 007.

"Patrick had a driver called Jock Frasier and a 'minder', for want of a better word, and a jeep with a bren machine gun on the bonnet and a lady friend up in Norway!"

Bill never saw Ian Fleming and only did what he modestly described as "run of the mill stuff…" But when pressed for more, he qualified it with a "run of the mill to you, but shocking to most of us."

He worked in small groups foraging for information. "You wouldn't know where you were going until you were picked and off you went. I volunteered to be the post corporal. That was the biggest mistake of my life."

Bill was given a jeep with orders to deliver messages no matter where the recipients were – all he had to do was find them. "It was a bit of a problem when they were 60 to 80 miles deep in hostile country. It was hairy sometimes. But you didn't think about it. We were just kids, daft kids."

Bill managed to evade capture, but was shot twice, the second time in the stomach, not while on a secret mission but walking down a street in the German town of Minden, hours before the war ended. They dug the bullet out and brought him back home. He married a girl whose mother ran a boarding house in Littlehampton and he stayed on in the town to live a more normal life in East Street. Any other old commandos still left in Littlehampton meet once a week at an angling club "and put the world to rights and all that sort of nonsense", was Bill's wry observation. I was about to leave the house in East Street when Bill told me to wait a minute. He went into his back garden, reappearing with a large bag of apples which he gave me as a parting gift.

Afterwards, I went to inspect a small sundial with a dedication to Bill's old unit in the grounds of Beach Crescent, where the old Beach Hotel and coffee house were before it. It was engraved with the words: "We will remember."

*

Among the 236 names engraved on the war memorial in Caffyn's Field was that of Private John Barnes, of 7th Battalion, Royal Sussex Regiment, 12th Division. Private Barnes' name had been on the Littlehampton memorial's roll-call from the start, even though he had been shot at dawn for desertion. Private Barnes had lived in Clun Road, where his mother

Sarah Jane and his father, Edward Barnes, had a house a few doors away. Now there was only one Barnes listed in the street in the census records at the Civic Centre, the executed soldier's nephew, Peter.

Ten minutes later, I was sitting with Peter and his wife Hazel drinking milky tea. They had invited me in without preamble, as if they were used to callers stopping by out of the blue and asking to hear the story of John Barnes, and perhaps, to an extent, they were.

"It was always a family skeleton in the cupboard. No one ever talked about it until after my father died," Peter told me.

A cousin had found out more from a man called Julian Putkowski, the author of *Shot at Dawn*, which told the story of the soldiers who were tried for desertion in the Great War. Between the war years of 1914 and 1918, 306 Tommies were executed by firing squad and a further 18 for cowardice.

Peter took out an old sepia photograph from a cupboard. "It's the only picture of him left," he said, handing it to me. It showed a young man in army cap and uniform, his hands hanging loosely at his side, eyes appearing to look slightly to one side of whoever had taken the picture. The photograph had been taken just after Private Barnes joined up as a volunteer in the recruitment drive of 1915.

While Hazel brought me yet another cup of milky tea, Peter took out the brooch that his grandmother, Sarah Jane Barnes, had always worn.

"She never took it off," he said.

I turned it around in my fingers. An integral part of the piece was a miniature version of the same sole surviving image of John Barnes in his uniform.

"He always used to go absent on a particular day of the year," sighed his nephew. "We don't know whether it was Grandmother's birthday or his parents' wedding anniversary, if he had a girlfriend or anything else."

The 24-year old had already asked to go on sick leave several times but had always been refused. The last time John went missing was from the Brown line trench near Arras on the Western Front. His absence was discovered in a roll-call at 1.15 am just before the men were due to go over the top.

They found him 50 miles away, walking in the town of Abbeville, looking conspicuous in his tin hat, still carrying his gas mask and bayonet.

"He asked where his unit was," Peter said, as we collectively considered the scene. "But because he didn't have his rifle anymore, he was charged with desertion."

The minute the young private threw his gun away, it was a capital offence, punishable by death.

Peter showed me the original charge sheets and witness statements from the court-martial, including John's own words: "As the bombardment was very severe, I became nervous and left the trench, moving towards Arras, where I slept the night."

The soldier's defence that he was suffering from battle stress was rejected without the consideration of any medical evidence and he was executed on July 4th, 1917.

"Sarah Jane, his mother, my grandmother, was chair of the Women's Legion. When she heard he'd been killed, she fought to get his name put on the cenotaph and on a memorial, just inside the west wing of Chichester Cathedral," said Peter.

Sarah Jane died in 1939, as a new world war was beginning. Another seventy years were to pass before all 306 Tommies gained a blanket pardon, after a test case brought by relatives of another soldier, Harry Farr. The date the test case came to court, said Hazel, had coincided with their fiftieth wedding anniversary.

"We were satisfied when they were all exonerated en block, but they should never have been shot," Peter concluded. He himself had served in the Royal Navy and said no one could know how they would react to the trenches of the First World War.

"Helps the families, doesn't it," said Hazel, chipping in, "but it doesn't do them any good."

It was a remote spot, but Peter's son Matthew had been to see John's grave in the Faubourg d'Arras cemetery. Private Barnes was buried in plot 4 J 17, beside another soldier, Private Robert Pattison of the 7th Queen's Regiment, who was shot on the same July morning in 1917.

21

Country Life in The Town

The dairy farmers of Wick had been farming in Littlehampton for a long time. The name 'Wick' or 'Whyke' is an Old English word for farm or dairy. Looking up 'Wick' in an Old English dictionary, I made other discoveries: 'Stanley' was a stone ley or field, 'treow' was a tree, and the origin of our modern English word for love was 'leof', meaning 'beloved'.

My walk with John Helyer, who had been born in Wick Farm Road and farmed dairy cattle for most of his life here, would be to crisp fallen leaves underfoot with an autumn nip in the air.

I was now lecturing one day a week at a university down the coast, to go with the freelance reporting I'd begun doing from my mother's shed for the same French radio station as before, this time reporting on British news from British soil, where the shed most certainly was.

John Helyer's family had come to England from Germany on a returning Cornish tin boat. The family were Lutherans, fleeing religious persecution under William III of Prussia. English farmland was expensive, so the men worked in tin mines in Dartmoor. Then word got around that the Duke of Norfolk was offering tenant farmers land rent-free for the first three years until the farmland was established. The family took up the offer and were soon farming sheep and dairy cattle in Littlehampton's green pastureland.

John's family had since moved from Wick Farm Road to East Road Farm in East Street, where a sign above the lintel informed the fire brigade they would be paid with the horseshoe still hanging there if they were ever called to the farm. I could almost hear Chance the fire dog's descendants barking.

I knocked.

John opened the door, looking every inch the gentleman farmer in his tweeds.

"Those were once all fields," John extended an arm, after we had set off. "The North and South Beaumont. We farmed all that land from the Worthing Road down to the sea. The cattle came up from Devon and were unloaded from their wagons at the railway station where drovers herded them down through the high street to whatever part of the farm we wanted."

When John was young, the cows were kept in the cellar. "If you had two or three cows then, you were a farmer," John explained. "Nobody had ten. We lived above them because the heat from the animals kept the place warm upstairs."

In the cool, northern end of the old farmhouse, the Helyers sold milk to Mortimer's Dairy in Littlehampton, the pails piled high into horse-drawn carts.

As a dairy man, John had risen at first light every morning for 19 years to feed his cows, without a day off, setting off on his tractor as the nuns were attending to their own morning ritual at St Joseph's Convent next door.

"You couldn't get a better neighbour – if we run out of anything, they've always got it for us," said John, as we walked. "When we have a party, you'd be surprised. One year we had some mistletoe and a sister grabbed hold of me and gave me a big kiss!"

That afternoon, John also told me about what had happened to his uncle Dick in the First World War. I had heard tragic wartime stories on my journey. Each one was poignant and moving and none more so than this: Private Richard Helyer's battalion had been ordered to go over the top and into No Man's Land and take a row of German trenches. Once secured, their orders were to attack the next enemy trench. The men successfully took the first but their runner was killed on the way to delivering the message; the line of communication to the British guns behind the men was severed. As the Tommies emerged from the first trench they had seized, the British guns opened up and young Dick Helyer went down in 'friendly' fire.

We turned into Green Lady Lane with its blue plaque at Lion Cottage, 57, East Street. A friend of a friend from an old Littlehampton family had told me the lane was named for the ghost of the green lady who haunted it. In fact it had been the home of the Green Lady Hostel with connections to the Suffragette Movement. Opened by Mary Neal and Emmaline Pethick in 1900, the hostel was a place for working-class girls to have a free holiday by the sea.

"Someone's burning leaves," I observed, sniffing the air, but John replied that it was just someone's dinner cooking, which set him on the theme of vegetables.

"Years ago we had a season. The broad beans came in, the peas came in. You had each vegetable at a certain time in the year. Now it's 'anywhen'. You can go and buy a runner bean or asparagus whenever you want."

I nodded, recalling how in France people ate dishes that still followed the seasons more closely than ours, with different summer, autumn and winter dishes.

We were following a well-worn path towards where the Helyer cows were once milked. You can follow it to Oakcroft Gardens where the old milking stalls were, all the way down to Thorncroft Road. We lingered at Cornfield Close, its name a legacy of those older days, not far from what John called the Long Meadows. He pointed, as if he could still see the fields opposite. "Every year, the circus used to come in there. They were very good. If there was any damage, they replaced it and paid for the hire of the field, because they knew if they didn't they wouldn't get anywhere to go next year."

We passed a children's playground that was once meadows used as horse paddocks, then the playing fields of what used to be Rosemead School, a private school for the children of Army officers.

"An officer only had to serve abroad and his children were educated," John said. "If they went abroad, their children went to the school free. Children from all over the world came here. The officers used to go and do a couple of months in Ireland to get the kids into the school."

Two or three cyclists snaked past us and I realised we were walking in what was now a cycle lane. A couple of small boys shouted "hello" from the branches of a tree.

"Little monkeys," John whistled. "I used to climb trees and get birds' eggs. When did you last see a Mistle thrush? You don't see them now."

There was an abundance of hawthorns studded with berries growing along the path, then a row of pre-war bungalows as we turned into Stanhope Road, a pleasant, leafy road that John could remember without a single car in the days when no one could afford one. Some of the houses in the street were immaculate, while others had gone to seed.

"Probably someone lived there all their life, getting old and living on their own, who just cannot afford to replace it," was John's observation.

One garden was full of borage leaves, twinkling with the herb's distinctive blue flowers once used as dressings for wounds. We passed a thatched barn used by the Helyers to store potatoes. "I was the last person to thatch that barn," John recalled. We went on past the police station, set well back from the road, then the convent which John said only kept its iron railings in the war because of the children living there.

"They used to come and take all your aluminium saucepans. But they didn't take railings away from schools. Everybody else lost theirs to the war effort." Except the basements near Ronnie Barker's home, I thought. On South Terrace metal bars over the cellars had been left to stop people falling in. Some of the metal was taken for armaments, but John thought a lot had been thrown away in the sea because it was only rough iron.

Now we were back in East Street with its pointed flint walls, fixed with mortar, lime and grit. You could see where some of the walls had been raised, with grey flint at the lower level. The flints had probably come from the beach, as they were smooth. The flints from the fields in the Helyers' farmhouse were knapped and square. The cottage walls had been cleaned with limewash to a buttery white, so different from the weathered grey I always associated with flint. Decorative stones or concrete caps had been laid on the top of the walls to stop the rain getting in. Building flint walls is a slow business. You do about four rows at a time and then have to let it settle.

*

I walked back down to the library afterwards with the town motto framed above the entrance, Progress. Now I prepared to test my own progress. I made my way down to the beach under clear skies, scrambling sideways down the shingle to where the tide was out, the line of the horizon almost imperceptible. Coils of sand and fronds of seaweed lay strewn about like garnish. There was hardly anyone around. I took a breath, and launched myself. I broke into a run without thinking about it, my arms out like an aeroplane, the mud soft enough to support my knees as I was running across the width of the beach from one groyne to the other and back again. Yes, I could do it. Again. I ran from end to end of the beach and back, a sense of power coursing through me, whooping and laughing like a mad woman as I went zig-zagging across the sand.

22

Bangers and Bonfires

I t was the last Saturday of October and the crowds had already begun to line St Catherine's Road, looking for a good position to watch the Bonfire Society's fireworks show later. The bonfire itself, on the beach, was being guarded round-the-clock. If vandals set light to it prematurely and the Fire Brigade had to come out, the Bonfire Society would have to foot the bill. Local jobbing gardeners had already contributed wood from old fences, leaves, and old palettes to the mound on East Green. This was Britain, land of health and safety regulations, and yellow rings had been drawn within which the bonfire had to be restricted, like a magic rite inside a pentangle.

Smugglers in days gone by had lit bonfires as warning beacons, but the practice had lost its criminal association with the formation of the Victorian Bonfire Society.

"It was a riotous affair, judging by the history accounts," Tyndall Jones had told me. "The Victorian love of naughty goings-on iced over with a veneer of respectability."

I had come with Mike, a friend who worked as a newspaper reporter in London, and Jah, jazz musician, former taxi driver and ex-grand vizier of Mouse Town. We joined the crowd inching its way like a single sentient organism down the High Street towards the sea front.

Jah, who had just had his flu jab and for some reason known only to him had come without a coat, was shivering. Our motley trio marched briskly to Arun Parade to warm ourselves with fish and chips before the show began. The queues were unreal. Fred's had the longer, so we plumped for Osca's.

Four girls, all with red hair, were serving. One of them, Lisa, said she had already gone through four pads of order sheets, with 100 sheets in each, and it was still only 7:30pm. Mine was the magic number 100.

There wasn't a table free when it was our turn at the counter so we ordered our cod and chips as a takeaway. As it arrived, a family finished their meal and we nabbed the empty table just by us. Poor Jah sank down gratefully for a moment. He was definitely in the wars. The food arrived and we beat a retreat to the wall outside overlooking the river to finish our supper there.

A funfair with a wailing ghost train was in full swing and vendors were wandering around hawking luminescent rabbits' ears, 'Star Wars' light sabres and illuminated wands with crystal balls on the top, as well as hot dogs and candy floss. I could hear snippets of exchanges, with people asking when the bonfire would be lit, when suddenly the procession hove into view. Decorated floats proclaiming themselves from Worthing, Crowborough and Taunton rolled ceremoniously down South Terrace, accompanied by marching cadets and brass bands. Steam rollers and old buses followed. Cheers and applause broke out. One man in the procession made a very convincing Johnny Depp dressed as Captain Jack Sparrow from *Pirates of the Caribbean*, with slanting kohl-ringed eyes and a flaming brand in his beringed fist.

One or two of the torches had been dropped in the road as the procession came on. As the last float went past, it was followed by a single unadorned police car.

"The bonfire's alight," cried Jah with relief, seeing a chance to warm himself up." Despite its bulk, it was already burning fast, spitting out sparks, the flames reflected in all the windows and fanlights of the villas lining South Terrace, so that it seemed they were aflame too. People were watching from their balconies. There were even spectators on scaffolding on some of the buildings.

As the first fireworks soared into the night sky, it began to rain. We crept closer to the furnace. The smell of fried onions and sparks drifted over carried in the salt breeze, the sound of the firework rockets reverberating off the walls of the buildings. By half-past-ten, it was all over – until next year – and we were back to the ordinary end of an October evening, all the cars quietly queueing to get out of the car park via the one way system.

On our way back to the car park, Mike, Jah and I paused at the war memorial as the procession had done earlier, as it does each year, so near Armistice Day. I shone a torch at the Bs. There was Private Barnes' name, right there.

23

On to the Horsham Road

The municipal cemetery is between the arms of Horsham Road and Worthing Road. I'd always intended to leave the Victorian cemetery – dilapidated and now closed – to near the end of my walk. I had arrived at that point. I wanted to find the grave of the Kitty O'Shea I had learned about in the history lessons of my girlhood.

Like Mrs O'Shea, my walking companion James Walsh, a GP for many years in Littlehampton, had a Liberal connection, and Irish blood like her beloved Parnell. James was accompanying me out of town and up the Horsham Road to the cemetery.

Our route was along East Street, running from what he said was called Smart's Corner – named after the Victorian chemist who ran the shop – near the Cuff Miller's Esso garage until it turned into the Horsham Road and the A259.

Together we passed the Georgian building of Winterton Lodge and its newer flats opposite the Ormsby Centre care home.

"Next to that are the ghastly modern excrescences of the police station and ambulance station in the one complex," said James, who didn't mince his words and had an incisive vocabulary. He had trained as a Surgeon Captain after joining the Navy as a sea cadet. "I first went to sea to convalesce after I had my appendix out as a 12-year-old," he said. "You could do that in those days."

I sympathised. I'd had mine out when I was nine and had been promised a chopper bike if I went through with the operation, which had never materialised!

James had a glamorous biography and sounded like another contender for James Bond. He had been caught up in the Icelandic Cod Wars before looking after Princess Margaret in the Seychelles and helping Prince Charles to water ski. On board ship, he also coached sailors in their English O-Level.

"Being a doctor is a great leveller, because you see all facets of humanity and conditions of the human spirit. On a ship you aren't only the doctor, but the confidante. The sailors come to you with their problems because they can't go to anyone else." He had also been director of Medical Reserves for the whole UK, in charge of 28 Royal Navy bases from Plymouth to Scotland, with a medical detachment trained for field and hospital ships in wartime.

We were passing Goda Road on our right. Before the Norman Invasion, Littlehampton had belonged to the sister of doddery old Edward the Confessor and the name of the countess lived on in a residential street.

"Anita Roddick and the Body Shop put Littlehampton on the modern commercial map," James was saying. "They started its renaissance and now there are other large industries like Littlehampton Welding and Dando Irrigation Drilling."

As a Littlehampton Harbour Commissioner, it had been one of James's pet ambitions to open up to the town centre with the riverside walkway. I was pleased to hear that, as a main consideration for my jigsaw journey had been to write how you could now walk through the town to the river and seafront. We continued along Horsham Road until we were level with Peregrine Road.

"I was given one of those houses when I came back from sea and started married life," James said, pointing to where the married quarters for officers and senior ratings – or non-commissioned officers – from the Royal Naval air station at Ford used to be, before the station was converted to a prison.

Peregrine Road led into Bell Davis Road, named after a famous submariner admiral. Esmonde Close was named in honour of a pilot James's father had known, a man who had been posthumously awarded the Victoria Cross for leading a raid by Swordfish planes on three German warships in the English Channel. But the Swordfish fighters were no match for the German guns and all perished, including Esmonde.

Littlehampton's maritime history was never far beneath the surface.

James told me about the Vietnamese Boat People.

"West Sussex took a lot in, about thirty or forty of the most wonderful people. Three generations – grandparents, parents and children, all of whom registered with my practice." The youngest generation now spoke perfect English, he said, and interpreted for their older relatives.

We were now north of Peregrine Road, the southern perimeter of the cemetery. I reminded the good doctor I intended to visit the grave of Kitty O'Shea. James' dark Irish eyes snapped.

"The moral climate of the time was that you were either married or you did not live with somebody," he said. "Charles Parnell was an Irishman and the Catholic morals of Ireland were possibly even stricter than Victorian London. She came here to get away from the hothouse of London or Dublin." The story had clearly animated him with his Irish grandfather and a Lord Mayor of Cork for a relative.

*

Kitty was a Victorian word for prostitute, the woman in the cemetery office told me. The nickname had been bandied about as an insult to Katharine O'Shea, a woman with distant blood ties to the British Crown who was mistress, then wife, then widow to Charles Parnell, the Irish Parliamentarian and campaigner for Home Rule.

Dawn Burns, who revealed herself as a sparky great-grandmother, had varnished nails and a feisty glint in her eye. She continued leafing through her index card system.

"Is it C or D con?" Dawn muttered inexplicably to herself as she began flicking through to find Kitty's grave. "So many names," she sighed. "So many people come asking, over the years. I've found an awful lot of graves for an awful lot of people." She cited a woman looking for a relative only to find he had been living in the area until just beforehand and his death had only just been announced.

"If only the relative had been in touch just a little sooner. I know you're here somewhere, you little devils." Dawn narrowed her eyes as her maroon nails flipped through the cards again. Just then, her colleague, Dean, returned to the office. That meant Dawn was now free to show me the grave. She knew the way by heart, but felt it was too complicated to give instructions without a grid reference. I followed the great-grandmother's brisk and purposeful stride into the darkness settling over the ranks of headstones. As we crossed the little car park, the site of the original chapel, I gave a quick glance across at the more recent church standing forlorn, sightless and abandoned a short way off, its arched windows filled in with concrete.

There, in the Catholic part of the cemetery, was Katharine's grave. A cruciform memorial stone inscribed to Katharine herself and her daughter was set to one side of the path. The inscription on the stone read 'fide et amore' – in faithfulness and love. The love affair with Parnell had ruined him, since he was only able to marry Katharine after her first husband, Captain William O'Shea, consented to divorce her. He had withheld his permission, some said, because he thought his wife would be the beneficiary of a rich aunt. Katharine had three daughters with Parnell, although one died while he was serving time in an Irish gaol. The affair was a scandal that must have animated drawing rooms and gentlemen's clubs from London to Dublin. The lovers defied their Catholic upbringing and the censure of their peers finally marrying some twenty miles away in Steyning. We know Katharine married Charles by special licence sometime between 9am and midday on June 25th, 1891 at the office of the Superintendent registrar of the Steyning Union, the registration district of Steyning.

But they had very little time together. Parnell's health had deteriorated from his time in and out of gaol addressing crowds in the rain on Irish Home Rule. He died less than four months after their wedding day at the age of just 45.

A small memorial plaque set up by the Parnell Society said it all:

'I will give my life to Ireland but to you I'll give my love.'

A single, small white feather fluttered down onto a nearby stone, under the winter-bare trees, sparse and stark, to the sound of distant traffic on the Worthing Road. Out there the rush hour was in force, the county's workforce heading home. It was always sobering to ponder the experiences of those who had lived turbulent lives in a quiet cemetery such as this.

Not far away in a space where the grass was neatly clipped were those whose lives had been brutally cut short by conflict. I read some of the headstones. Unknown airmen and sailors from Britain, Canada and Australia, along with German prisoners-of-war were remembered. One grave simply said: 'Ein Deutscher Soldat' – 'A German soldier'.

24

Nuns, pies and Victoria sponge cake

My bicycle was stashed and padlocked up in the cycle rack at Littlehampton station. It was a city bike with a comfort saddle. I could now ride again, though my right knee still ached after longer trips. Time had gone by. I could walk in heels again. I still carried my tens machine with me as much a talisman as an emergency back-up, along with a little pot of the pungent tiger balm, an ointment made with camphor and other herb oils to warm the muscles, that Neil in the gym had recommended.

The hem of my combat trousers was saturated, but I was on a mission, as I crossed Franciscan Way with the trolley at the traffic lights. It was December and I was pushing a trolley borrowed from Littlehampton's new Waitrose, guiding it over cobbles and tarmac slick with rain. Inside the trolley were boxes of Victoria sponge cream cakes, mince pies and Roses chocolates. The cakes and chocolates were an early Christmas present for the nuns of St Joseph.

This wasn't my first visit to St Joseph's, nor the second. Both previous times I had immediately been invited in to share the nuns' supper, first of soup and fish fingers, then of macaroni cheese, so that it became a running joke between us that I always wanted to come over on a Friday for fish fingers. The nuns were friendly, down-to-earth and generous; they had been here a long time running a children's home since Franciscan missionaries first arrived here more than a century ago. There was also a nursing home for elderly people in the grounds of the convent.

I had warmed at once to Sister Anastasia McGonigal, that first time. She had sat me down in a high wing-backed chair in a small parlour near the refectory.

"The building had been damaged during the war and had to be rebuilt," she said in the slightly quavering voice with its lilting accent that belied a forceful character.

"The Government wanted family groups. Some of the children had nobody. Some did have family, but because the parents were working or because they were caught up in the war, they had to send the children away. Later on, nursing was in great need in Littlehampton because the children had grown up and needed care in their old age. But there were very few nursing homes."

There had been 100 boys and seventy girls at St Jo's, from all over, she said, from Spain, from the north of England, from London, babies and children right up to 14, the school-leaving age back then, when they had to find a job and make their own way in the world.

"But the beautiful thing is, there was no distinction made between them and they never made distinctions themselves. They were one big happy family," the sister said with a smile.

"I remember one child who came as a baby who had rickets and was very badly deformed. The sisters used to massage him and do exercises with him. And do you know, that boy came back for our centenary anniversary and he was so, so grateful for what was given to him through this convent that he presented us with a silver dish."

"Has anyone else ever come back again?" I had asked her.

She nodded. "Many." A sense of serenity and grace radiated from Sister Anastasia. "Can you 'find the record of my mum?', or 'when was I there?' or 'who left me?' or 'who paid for me?' But often we didn't get any money."

Some children were traumatised after being taken away from their parents, or not having any, Sister Anastasia said.

"The boy with rickets," she recalled. "I tried to find his mum and he thought he'd found her and it turned out to be a wild goose chase. He was so, so traumatised by that. Thank God he was able to come back and talk about it with us."

I had quite a few friends who had tried to find their natural parents. One was a policeman whose father was a merchant seaman. Another had been adopted into a family of four after her mother, a girl of 15, had given birth. For years, she had tried to meet her mother, lodging her official request every 10 years as she was required to do, only to be rejected. I remembered her anguish and heartache and my surprise when she told me that history had repeated itself and that at 15 she had given

154

up a baby girl for adoption. But her experience meant that when her own daughter sought her out, she had immediately agreed. And when she herself was 50, her real mum had finally agreed to see her.

In many ways, Sister Anastasia had been a mother or sister to the children. She herself had taken Holy Orders when she was 17, leaving the peninsular of Inishowen in County Donegal, for St Joseph's.

The nun told me: "I had two sisters already in the congregation. I knew everyone and I just wanted to come." As a young girl, she left home knowing she might not see her own family again, since there were no holidays and the convent could not afford to send them home. "We weren't soft – times were tough," she said. "Everything we had, everything we did was for the children. I thank God that He gave us the grace to make these sacrifices for the children."

The convent has started holding reunions. Sister Anastasia thinks today is worse than the 1950s when she first came to the town and no one had anything. "Now there are the 'haves' and 'have-nots'. Now you have some people who've got a lot and others who don't know how to manage. We've brought a group of people up and they don't know how to care for a home or a family. They don't know how to make do with the basics. That's the difference. During the War, people didn't have much, but they all pulled together. There wasn't competition, people trying to outdo the other, like there is now."

Sister Anastasia had spent more than 40 years in Littlehampton. It was her home and she liked to go into the convent garden to be quiet. She loves the sea, "especially on a windy, blowy day with the waves. It just does something for me."

"Do you wish you'd married, maybe had children and grandchildren of your own?" I asked her that night.

"If the Lord wants you on a special path, then he gives you the necessary grace to cope with whatever comes your way," was her answer. "If I had to live my life again, I would do exactly the same. I have been totally fulfilled. I am able to have relationships, but not where the person controls me. I enter into a relationship freely."

It had been the frankest personal discussion I've ever had with a nun. I thought about it now as I wheeled the Waitrose trolley onto the driveway of St Joseph's and pressed the bell of the convent's double front doors. The rain was showing no sign of letting up and I still had to collect my bike and cycle back to my garden room home.

"I'll murder ya!" shouted the sister who opened the door, on seeing the laden trolley, saying it over several times, her sweet, round face breaking into a huge smile. She and three other sisters each planted kisses on my cheek and hugged me in delight at their Christmas presents. They are good women who live frugally and I was pleased to get them something they would not have bought themselves. I wished them goodnight and wondered if there would be another party with mistletoe with their neighbours, the Helyers, like in other years before.

I returned the trolley to the supermarket, thanking them for the favour. Tucking the bedraggled hems of my trousers into fluorescent clips and easing on my high-visibility jacket, I fetched down my bike from the rack, fiddling with the annoying clasp on my helmet, then began cycling back home, accepting I would be drenched when I arrived. However, once you have accepted it, it is exhilarating riding in the rain, with the thought of a long, hot shower at the other end.

25

Wyrms and water dragons

It was little more than a week before Christmas and there was still one last quest to accomplish in my jigsaw journey across town.

It was time to go dragon hunting.

It wasn't the first time I had tried to meet up with the local historian the vicar had put me in touch with after the farmhand, George Carmen. Once I had tried to keep a rendezvous with Alan Burnett, the historian, at the parish church at Lyminster, but got caught up with hundreds of drivers in a terrible traffic jam and had to ring the vicar as an intermediary to postpone it.

Now it was Christmas Eve and the year was nearly at an end. I'd kissed my mother's garden room goodbye and was living independently – or as much as you can when you are renting the house next door.

I drove past the George & Dragon at Burpham, signposted off the main road. At Crossbush, I followed the winding road as it looped south, passing the Astracats boarding house before I turned into Church Lane.

The church of St Mary Magdalene was built on what used to be a Saxon nunnery, where two Benedictine nuns had laid the foundations of Christianity here on this spot. This was where Athelstan, the ancient King of Wessex, had held court 900 years ago in a royal barn in the nearby copse. It had served as the rural seat of his 'Witan' or court that dealt with problems in the area. Was it possible that Knucker and a rumour of the dragon marauding sheep had been one of those problems laid before the royal court?

Winter light lay across the broad, green fields falling away to the north so they seemed to gleam in the low afternoon sun. Some way off, a London-bound train whooshed by on its purposeful way.

I shook hands with Alan over the lynch gate of the church, he on one side of the gate, me standing on the other with my feet in the lane still called the old Driftway. For centuries, the cattle and sheep were driven from the byres along here to market in Chichester, 13 or so miles and four or five hours droving away. The Driftway was now a glistening muddy track, arcing across the fields to run all the way from the Poling marshes along what was nowadays Church Road, past the Knucker Hole, to Ford, where livestock was traditionally herded across the Arun valley. Pilgrims, as well as drovers, had used this route to travel the South Downs, seeking out the spire of Chichester Cathedral to guide them, the first spire visible also to those at sea. There were other marine links too. Many of the fields and meadows here are reclaimed from the sea, with the result that the soil is rich in minerals.

"At high tide the sea once lapped the walls of the church," Alan said. "Ships came in. Danes came in. When the tide went out, there were salt pans that made Lyminster such a rich parish. In the Domesday Book, it was rated even higher than Chichester with all its Roman heritage, because of the salt." Alan looked down at his shoes, "We'd best walk down through the churchyard."

We picked our way through the gravestones, down towards the path leading towards the Knucker Hole. It seemed to me that perhaps this was a tale of those age-old companions, good and evil: Where there's a chapel, you usually find gargoyles. Perhaps Knucker was some kind of gargoyle in his cold, deep pool, once used for growing watercress.

Alan confirmed the pool had been sold to a group who used it mostly for fishing, as I'd learned in that phone call back in the summer. It did indeed belong to the owners of a nearby house. We knocked at its front door, but there was no reply. People had asked about access, but the owners were reluctant to agree "for health and safety reasons," said Alan: after all, the Knucker Hole was very deep. "It's a shame. It's a lovely spot and there are rumoured to be otters."

We passed seats for people walking the Downs, made out of footstones from when the churchyard was tidied a few years ago.

Alan said conversationally as I followed him: "The children

always ask, 'Is there a dragon there now?' I had a lady visit the church from Wales. She runs a dragon museum and has a collection of dragons from all over. She took all the details of ours, plus any pictures we had."

As we walked, heading towards a glint of water peeping through trees in the distance, we came up with suggestions for how the dragon yarn – if yarn it was – might have first been spun.

I offered my own theory: "A gullible or short-sighted peasant saw something, maybe a sea eagle stealing a lamb, but not knowing what it was, said it was a dragon."

My hand shot out instinctively as Alan nearly slipped in his unsuitable footwear, just as we arrived at the dragon's den. I saw the sparkle of fickle sun on water through the gaps in a wire fence, ringed by willow trees. The pool was almost entirely hidden by the willows and undergrowth that had grown using the wire barricade as a trellis.

There was a sense of being out of time. We were two credulous villagers from an older age approaching the pool, perhaps with an offering to pacify the fearful beast that we believed had been pilfering our lambs. Or even a poisoned pie as Jim Pulk or Puttock and the knight had done.

But of the dragon, there was no sign.

There was other wildlife, though. The burrs of the briars pressed their prickles into my coat as I peered through the wire. The briars hung down like lazily festooned cobwebs, nature's party-streamers and tinsel hung out for Christmas. But Alan said it was the best view he had ever seen of the pool, without the trees in leaf. There was a small lake and another patch of water, a strip of land between them with small islets crowded with shelduck and mallards all jostling for space. I had been warned not to upset the ducks. They had begun honking vigorously as we approached.

It looked like they were upset.

"It's a marvellous place for blackberries in the summer," Alan remarked, "it's full of them."

I thought about how the men of Lyminster had once taken the six bell ropes from their church tower and lowered them, tied end-to-end, into the Knucker Hole without reaching the bottom. More recently, divers had gone down and found the Hole was fed by five chalk streams at the base. I now knew there were other such Holes in the county – in Worthing, Lancing and Shoreham, all fed by springs – hence the belief they were bottomless.

"Which is why it never freezes over. It's moving water," explained Alan. "But when it's very cold, a vapour hovers over it – like the breath of a dragon."

A great yew tree, storm-blasted and lopsided, had been forced to grow at an angle of 45 degrees pointing towards the old pilgrim's way.

We bent under its overhanging branches, keeping to the path passing the houses that had once been the homes of the first man to break the four-minute mile, Roger Bannister, and author Rosemary Anne Sisson and her Cambridge professor father. A steel girder had been used to make a small bridge across the end part of the pond outside the wire fencing, for walkers heading across the Downs to Arundel. It was full of winter-dried bulrushes that were choking this bit of the pond. I climbed over a stile and looked across at Arundel Castle and Cathedral on the other side of the valley. Alan had never walked beyond the small bridge. If you carry on in the footsteps of the medieval pilgrims nowadays, across the fields, skirting Crossbush, you can buy a burger at McDonald's, emerging at Arundel station.

Suddenly Alan piped up: "What the heck is that? There, in the field?" For a split second, I thought we'd found our dragon after all. "Knucker?" I asked in a whisper.

"Are those sheep grazing?" Alan pointed.

I laughed. "If they are, they are sheep with long necks!"

And as we moved nearer, we saw we were on the borders of the oddest kingdom of all. A colony of swans was feeding on the vegetation, bending their necks deep into the foliage. There were at least 100 of them. Alan, who lived and liked to walk here often, had never seen the swans before. But then he had never crossed the makeshift bridge.

I touched the top wire of the fence with a gloved hand. "Is it electrified?" I asked a second later. It was one of the stupidest things I had done, but fortunately the fence was not.

We left the swans and took the Driftway back, trying to avoid the puddles, but our shoes were very soon coated with mud. Alan explained how, in 1643, during the English Civil War when Arundel Castle was besieged, the dead were loaded into farm carts and brought to the church here and buried just outside the south wall. Bones had been dug up years ago and unfortunately discarded. A more recent excavation revealed a mass grave, with the bodies laid out in a religious fashion, including a mother and child. Alan thought they had probably come from the barracks at Crossbush.

*

At the church, it looked like the vicar had given Alan the wrong keys. A casual observer would have thought we were trying to break in, as after a struggle, we made an unorthodox entry through the vestry door. There was a poster designed and painted by Alan himself on the wall, of a map with an owl and a pussycat, and a pig for good measure, since Edward Lear had written his poem *The Owl and the Pussycat* while unsuccessfully courting a lady in Arundel.

A panel of coloured glass inside the church showed morning and night scenes of a dragon being hunted down. Close by was a stone lid, the one said to be the gravestone of the knight who had felled Knucker and cut off the monster's head. I could just make out the carved shape of a knight's sword and hilt where the stone hands would have rested. There was no inscription. But a paper booklet in the church informed us that the cross over the herringbone pattern on the lid symbolised the hero's sword against the dragon's ribs. Even though I now knew there had been no such thing as Knucker ... didn't I?

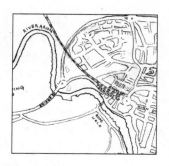

26

Full Circle

It was a few days later and tiny soft flakes of snow were whirling to the ground in the freezing north-easterly wind. A yoga class I had begun attending was cancelled due to the weather. A row of icicles hung off the pitched roof of the garden shed in the lee of the fence on the other side of which was my mother's house. Cars were still snowed in but I had bought myself a pair of yak tracks, each a mesh of steel coils that slipped on over my walking boots. With them I could walk confidently over compacted snow and ice.

Inside the pub was warmth, laughter and quiet chatter. Tinsel hung in loops from the beams and a baby Christmas tree, swaddled in fairy lights, was cheerfully changing colour like a chameleon on the bar counter.

The jigsaw journey was over – though, I had a feeling that, in a sense, I'd always be walking it. It had been a pilgrimage, not to a cathedral in Spain, but following some road of my own. Perhaps another year I would put on my pilgrim's walking boots and head for St James of Compostela.

With night pressing against the mullioned window panes of the pub, I bought a bottle of the beer I had been promising myself I would try only at this point, when I had finished my walk through town. It was a dark and enigmatic beverage, brewed locally in Ford; a dragon's brew no less. I carried the bottle and a glass over to a corner snug, as a church clock chimed the winter hour out in the darkness.

Sitting there on my own, I reflected on my jigsaw journey across and through Littlehampton. I thought of the friends I had made along the way. Gary and his circus and painted ponies, Alan and his pet chicken, the Mayor of Mewsbrook Park, the wonderful Sister Anastasia so full of grace, Lilias flying her freak flag, Staci and Dave and Jah and his beloved music and all of them with their stories: of Chance the fire brigade dog, the whiskered and battle-scarred mouser, Able Seaman Simon; and a haze, like dragon's breath coming off the pool on chill mornings as the water flowed, as it had always done, through the Downs to surface in the Knucker Hole.

A dark, old ale with a malt and fruit aroma, said the label with its picture of a knight flourishing his sword and spear at a roaring dragon. I poured my beer and, before I took a sip, rather theatrically raised my glass to toast all that a town on the Sussex coast on the way to nowhere had brought me.

I had finished writing up my jigsaw journal at around 1 in the morning on Christmas Day. But, in fact, I wasn't quite finished. There was still a piece to add. When I had first pitched up at Littlehampton, it had been on a number 700 bus, then by car and later on my bike. I hadn't yet walked down the long road from the big Tesco roundabout as I'd wanted. It felt right to walk that stretch before I could truly say I was finished. That time was nigh!

The morning was crisp, bright and wintry, not unlike the one when I'd first gone exploring on West Beach. I parked up and set off down Terminus Road, past the station, towards Bridge Road heading out of town.

One new thing I have learned from walking through Littlehampton is that, however well or little you know a place, there are always interesting nooks and crannies in amongst the ordinary that you didn't know about. Something not on any tourist trail or a few hundred yards from where you live, an unexpected piece of history about someone or something, ready to reveal itself, if you just chipped away slightly at the surface.

Walking down Bridge Road, I noticed a little memorial plaque embedded in a wall in a new block of flats, dedicated to four men who had died in the Great War: a Royal Engineer and sergeants from the Rifle Brigade, the Somerset Yeomanry and the Royal Sussex Regiment, who had all made the ultimate sacrifice.

I walked on past the Steam Packet and the Arun View pubs, the cycle lane and the Harbour Board workshop. I could smell the pungent smell of asphalt from the factory making tarmac from the granite chippings that are still unloaded in Littlehampton Harbour. I crossed the road. A path led to the superstore and a footbridge across the railway tracks to the gas station. It is here that a signpost welcomes you to Littlehampton, twinned with Chennevières-sur-Marne in France and the German town of Durmersheim. There is a warning about rabies and directions to the river and seafront, the youth hostel, the town centre and a stone's throw away, the stop for the number 700 bus.

Note from the author

I would like to extend a sincere thank you to everyone who contributed to this little travelogue. A special mention must go to the Deputy Town Clerk Rosie Parfitt and Councillor Alan Gammon of Littlehampton Town Council; also to Juliet Thomas, Curator of Littlehampton Museum; Mike Brooke for photography on a winter beach; Andy Hammond and Tracey West for proofreading; historian Dr Ian Friel and coastal engineer Roger Spencer for their information on the river Arun and Eric Benham for the lowdown on Lily Savage and cinemas – a potent combination! I am indebted also to Gary Smart for his insight and to Andy Kille for practical advice. Also to Michael Walsh, my publisher, for his patience and professionalism. To everyone within the pages and without, who contributed with your interest, experience and knowledge of Littlehampton – thank you.

I would also like to pay tribute to the late Gwen Eggleston of Littlehampton's Local History Society, who helped me get started.

Maps and archive material reproduced by kind permission from Littlehampton Museum and Arun District Council.

This book has been part-funded by Littlehampton Town Council as part of its Arts Initiative Programme. The views and comments are those of the author alone and are not necessarily shared by Littlehampton Town Council.

Alis Moss.

Reprinted from

𝕷𝖎𝖙𝖙𝖑𝖊𝖍𝖆𝖒𝖕𝖙𝖔𝖓 𝕲𝖆𝖟𝖊𝖙𝖙𝖊

NOVEMBER 10th, 1944.

AIR RAIDS ON LITTLEHAMPTON

Official Map And Figures of Every Incident

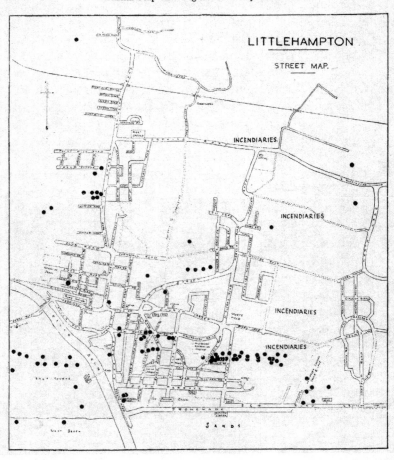

LITTLEHAMPTON

STREET MAP.

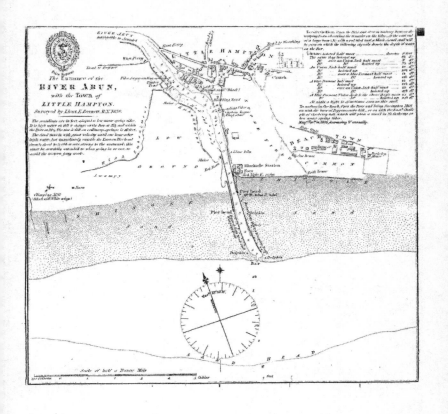

opposite: Air raids in 1944 as reported in the *Littlehampton Gazette*.

above: Littlehampton and the River Arun, as surveyed by Lieutenant E. Barnett of the Royal Navy in 1830.

overleaf: Ship and aviation wrecks located off the coast at Littlehampton.

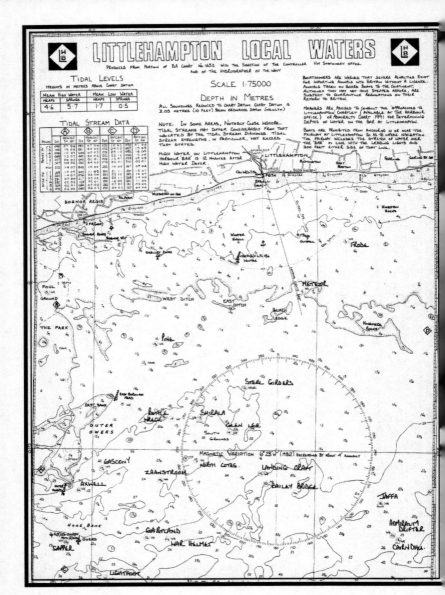

Littlehampton
Town Council

Littlehampton dates for your diary

June   Armed Forces Day
July   Littlehampton Carnival
September   Town Show and Family Fun Day
October   Littlehampton Bonfire Celebrations
December   Lights On event

Useful info for travellers near and far

Littlehampton Youth Hostel
61-63 Surrey St,
Littlehampton,
West Sussex
BN17 5AW
Tel: 0845 371 9670
www.yha.org.uk/hostel/littlehampton

Littlehampton Library
Maltravers Road,
Littlehampton
BN17 5NA
Tel: 01903 716450

Littlehampton Town Council and Museum
Manor House,
Church Street,
Littlehampton
BN17 5EW
Tel: 01903 738100
www.littlehampton-tc.gov.uk

The Look and Sea Visitor Centre
61-63 Surrey Street,
Littlehampton
BN17 5AW
Tel: 01903 718984
www.lookandsea.co.uk

Wickbourne Family and Children Centre
Clun Road,
Littlehampton
BN17 7DZ
Tel: 01903 276840